PRT0314A

Printed in the United States

ISBN-13: 9781620866474
ISBN-10: 1620866471

www.mascotbooks.com

THE LEPRECHAUN's
GAME DAY RULES

Sherri Graves Smith

Illustrated by Damon Danielson

I'm Leprechaun and welcome to Notre Dame!
I am the proud mascot of this school that has legendary football fame!

You can show your school pride in a special way,
just follow these simple rules on our big game day!

It is polite to greet those you meet
with a friendly "hi" or "hello."
But don't go to strangers alone.
Try it first with someone you know!

Remember, it is nice to share with others,
not just your sisters or brothers.

If someone does something kind,
a simple "thank you" will do just fine.

If you need help or a special favor,
use the word "please" with your friend or neighbor.

If you help someone, and they say "thanks" to you,
just say "you're welcome." It's the right thing to do.

Remember before you enter the game,
clean the spot from where you came.

Whether you are five or seventeen,
you can always help someone in need.

When you're standing in a line,
it is best to take your time.

Patience is something you will learn,
when you kindly wait your turn.

It can be very crowded in the stands.
Please be careful and hold your parent's hand.

If you step on someone's feet
on the way to your seat,
"excuse me" or "I'm sorry" will do
when asking someone to pardon you.

Remember it is thoughtful to say,
"you're forgiven" or "that's okay."

Before the National Anthem starts,
take caps off heads and put hands on hearts.

If a player makes a mistake,
it's never a reason to act with hate.

When a play goes very well,
it's good to say the player's swell.

It is great to love our school,
but to our rivals, don't be cruel.

It is okay to celebrate and cheer with fans,
just be close to your parents in the stands.

It is even okay to jump around,
just do not knock someone down.

If the ref's call is not for us,
it's not right to shout and fuss.

If the ref's call puts us in first place,
let's not rub it in our opponent's face.

Even though players tackle hard
to keep others from gaining yards,
be sure to watch them interact carefully.
Players help each other and try not to bully.

When you watch the Fighting Irish Band,
it is nice to clap for them in the stands.

If the other team does win,
remember, you will play again!

If our team comes out on top,
it is great to cheer a lot!
But a sore winner, you should never be.
Winning is not a reason to be mean.

If you want to see good sportsmanship and have some time to wait,
at the end of the game, look midfield to watch the teams congratulate.

Thanks for listening to some rules
on minding manners at our school.

Goodbye, my Fighting Irish fan!
Come back soon to cheer with me in the stands!

The End

Check out these other *Game Day* titles from Sherri Graves Smith and Mascot Books:

-*Albert and Alberta's Game Day Rules* (Florida)

-*Big Al's Game Day Rules* (Alabama)

-*Mike the Tiger's Game Day Rules* (LSU)

-*Buzz's Game Day Rules* (Georgia Tech)

-*Cimarron's Game Day Rules* (Florida State)

-*Hairy Dawg's Game Day Rules* (Georgia)

-*Rameses' Game Day Rules* (North Carolina)

-*Aubie's Game Day Rules* (Auburn)

-*Smokey's Game Day Rules* (Tennessee)

-*Cocky's Game Day Rules* (South Carolina)

-*Tiger's Game Day Rules* (Clemson)

-*Reveille's Game Day Rules* (Texas A&M)

-*Bully's Game Day Rules* (Mississippi State)

-*Nittany Lion's Game Day Rules* (Penn State)

-*Go Blue's Game Day Rules* (Michigan)

-*Big Red's Game Day Rules* (Arkansas)

-*Truman's Game Day Rules* (Missouri)

-*Blue Devil's Game Day Rules* (Duke)

-*Brutus Buckeye's Game Day Rules* (Ohio State)

-*Wildcat and Scratch's Game Day Rules* (Kentucky)

-*Rebel's Game Day Rules* (Mississippi)

More to come!

Visit www.GameDayRules.com

for more information.

A Note from the Author

Photo © Sara Hanna Photography. www.SaraHanna.com. The photo was taken at the Swan Coach House.

Sports are more than just a form of exciting entertainment or even a great way to exercise. Sports are a fantastic way to build self-esteem and bring together a sense of community that crosses gender, race, age, economic, social, and even religious lines.

There are many important life lessons that can be learned through sports – how to win AND to lose with grace, being a team player, learning from mistakes, civility towards opposing teams, playing by the rules, respecting the decisions made by the officials – to just name a few. Those skills can be translated into the classroom, the board room, and even in handling the everyday ups and downs of life.

In writing this pledge, it is my goal to instill the solid values of competing with respect, dignity, and integrity in our children, our nation's greatest asset.

-Sherri

SPORTSMANSHIP
PLEDGE

LEARN

I will learn how to play the sport, like running and catching the ball.
Learning how to play is great, but having fun is best of all!

EXCELLENCE

I will strive for excellence and live to the best of my best potential.
Doing the best you can is always an essential!

GROWTH

I will exercise my body and the brain in my head.
It is important that they are healthy and that I keep them both well-fed!

INTEGRITY

I will be respectful, honest, and fair, and play according to the rules.
I will behave this way whether at play, at home, or at school!

TEAMWORK

Each member of the team is important, whether coach, player, or me.
I will support them and do my part so we can be the best that we can be!

PLEDGE OF SUPPORT

The Sportsmanship Pledge is an important foundation upon which I will foster and build.
I will be an example and show leadership in this pledge whether on or off the field!

water color,
gouache, and
casein painting

studio publications, inc.

in association with

THOMAS Y. CROWELL COMPANY

New York and London

by Adolf Dehn

water color,

gouache, and

casein painting

contents

L

Acknowledgments

The author wishes to thank the museums, private collectors, and the Associated American Artists, who have permitted works to be reproduced in these pages; John Schiff, who photographed most of the author's work; and the five great American artists who have contributed notes at the end of this book.

introduction

A MAJOR DEVELOPMENT IN THE ART WORLD DURING THE PAST TEN YEARS OR SO IS THE staggering increase in the number of people who are painting, and the other hundreds of thousands who want to paint. Not only do corporation executives and lawyers paint, but so do butchers, bakers, movie actors and actresses. And a gentle old lady of ninety is quite as famous for her painting as a world-renowned prime minister and a president of the United States. It is certainly a healthy sign, this rebellion against serfdom to the machine.

The popular interest in art that exists today explains why so many books attempting to tell how to paint water colors and oils have been presented to the public. Most books, including my own, in the former category have dealt only with transparent water color, and the publishers have asked me to write a new and different book involving not only the transparent technique, but also the related and increasingly popular gouache and casein methods. It has been my aim to present this information as simply and clearly as possible so that every reader can learn, step by step, each method. Advanced students and practicing artists, too, may discover several new ideas and approaches which might prove stimulating.

Until quite recently water coloring was too often a neat little affair of floating and flooding some pretty washes on a white paper. The results were frequently ingratiating in their own delicate way, but many dabblers worshiped transparency so much that their rocks and hills had no more weight than a summer sky and their shadows were blue or lavender to the point of nausea. These water colorists knew little about structure and design and whatever strong emotion they may have had about nature was lost in their adoration of thin-bodied aquarelle. Oil painters spoke slightingly of the medium, many would not touch it, and at best others would flirt with it briefly, and never, never, turn in a serious painting.

This state of affairs has changed radically in the past dozen years. New concepts of design, color, and techniques, as well as new ideas of what a work of art really is, have broken down many barriers; the artist today dares to use any and all mediums, separately and together in entirely new ways.

Never forgetting that transparent water color is, or at least can be, an incomparable and beautiful medium, we can go on to study gouache and the even more opaque casein. In passing, let it be said that gouache is centuries old; but artists of our time have rediscovered her, and the paint manufacturers' claim that they have given her new blood and new life is proving to be true.

This book presents transparent water color, or aquarelle, first. After working through this section the reader should have sufficient knowledge and experience to make an easy transition to gouache and finally to casein colors, building a thick impasto comparable to oils.

A first reading of the exercises may sound rather formidable, but if you exercise a little patience, I can guarantee you will spend some fascinating hours of work. I do not spend too much time explaining; instead I tell you to *do*, for in doing you will learn far more than through endless pages of discussion. An instructor, by his own enthusiasm and love of his subject, can stimulate his pupils to greater endeavor. Although this personal contact must be lacking in a book, I hope somehow, in and between the lines, I can engender in the reader the combination of passion and patience that every artist should possess.

At the start, some people get into a state wondering whether or not they have talent. If they must dwell on it at all, I vigorously urge them to assume they have none. Then they can happily proceed as amateurs, out to enjoy the whole business of painting and, from there, climb the ladder as far as they are prepared to go.

Finally, may I suggest you make it a practice to go to museums and galleries and study the best works of the past and the present. Or, if they are not easily accessible, browse through the hundreds of books that have been published on master works. With study and enjoyment of all types of art comes new stimulation and growth in every artists' painting. Make it a point especially to see the great water colors all the way from the Chinese to the early English and all of our contemporaries.

materials and equipment for

water-color painting

THE STUDENT, LIKE THE PROFESSIONAL, SHOULD CERTAINLY USE THE BEST PAPERS, brushes, and colors that he can find. No one can produce his best work if he is hampered by inferior materials. An artist needs all the encouragement he can get, so let him at least be confident in his basic equipment.

In listing items in this chapter, I have added a few general notes on handling and usage which may be worth referring back to from time to time; especially the notes at the end of the chapter on rather unorthodox procedures with certain less basic equipment like sandpaper, rubber cement, and wax crayons, which it will not be necessary to elaborate upon in later chapters.

COLORS

Among the best makes of transparent water colors the following are well known and readily available: Winsor & Newton, Grumbacher (Schminke), Weber, Devoe, and Rembrandt. Usually they are listed in four categories:

A.—Absolutely permanent   C.—Moderately durable
B.—Durable   D.—Fugitive

For the average palette enough colors can be found under the permanent and durable categories. Many artists avoid the fugitive colors entirely, and I think it a good idea. However, in commercial jobs where brilliance is necessary and permanence is of secondary importance, fugitive colors serve their purpose well.

Water-color paints come in tubes and small pans. I recommend the former for general use. Tubes keep the pigment soft, saving time when mixing quantities of color for large areas; the moist colors can also be used directly from the tubes for powerful accents and contrasts in a water color. Pan colors need more moistening with water to get the full strength. They are good for small and delicate pictures or for quick little outdoor sketches. Their great advantage is that they are handily packed and easy to carry.

Here is a basic list of colors that I recommend you have on hand:

Yellow Ochre (A)   Cobalt Blue (A)
Naples Yellow (B)   French Ultramarine (A)
Cadmium Yellow (A)   Burnt Sienna (A)
Hooker's Green No. 2 (B)   Warm Sepia (B)
Chromium Oxide Green (Dull) (A) Payne's Gray (B)
Vermilion (A)   Black, Ivory, and Lamp
Alizarin Crimson (B)   Black (A)
Opaque White, such as Aero White in a jar, or Titanium White
      (Shiva Casein)

(The colors are all Winsor & Newton except the Chromium Oxide Green and Payne's Grey, which are put out by Schmincke.)

When you have had experience with these colors, you may wish to add Indian or Venetian red, lemon yellow, Prussian blue, and experiment with others.

The palette will vary greatly according to the type and size of the water color; it will probably vary with your mood, too. Sometimes I use only five or six of the colors listed above; sometimes, nearly all of them. At other times, new colors suddenly appeal to me, and I try them out with the old palette or with an entirely new one. This continuous experimenting with new colors and combinations is one of the great excitements of painting, and every artist must eventually arrive at his own preferences through trial and error.

When a cap dries stiffly onto a tube, it may be loosened by holding a lighted match under it for a few seconds. The cap should unscrew easily. Be sure to screw the caps on the tubes immediately after use; otherwise the tube will dry out. If it does this, throw it away. There is no use trying to get color out of a dead tube.

WATER-COLOR BOXES

For indoor painting a water-color box is not necessary. Actually, I don't own one at all, but for those who wish one for outdoor excursions, I recommend a large metal water-color box. Tubes can be easily and neatly stored in a suitably shaped wood or tin box (such as a cigar box or oblong cooky tin), or in a work table drawer. You may find a long narrow tin tray or a piece of board convenient for setting out your tube colors while working at home. Or you may simply arrange them on a piece of newspaper on the table around your palette. Brushes may be stored, bristles upward, in a jar; plastic and tin containers are available for carrying them. Always wash your brushes thoroughly in water after use; shape each brush to a nice thin point, and never let anything lean against or weigh on the bristles.

PALETTE

The simplest palette is a large white plate. I use two of them—one for black, Payne's gray, blues, and greens; the other for yellows, reds, and browns. When the plate gets too dirty, wipe it clean with moist tissues. After you have finished for the day, the plate can be held under the faucet and washed off with a large brush. Large blobs of color that have dried to the plate may be left and used again. A large porcelain tray, a slab of white marble, or a pie tin can also be used as a palette. Some artists use a square of glass, but it is easier to see the colors on a smooth white surface.

BRUSHES

You may at first be shocked at the price of the best large-sized water-color brushes, but don't think that you are saving money by getting a cheap one. An inferior brush won't last; the hairs will fall out at the most inconvenient moments, and the brush will not behave. To avoid unnecessary difficulties, I urge you to try a few of the very best brushes. If they are cleaned carefully after each use, good brushes will last long enough to be economical in comparison to the inferior ones. Besides the durability of a good brush, the artist gets a craftsman's joy in handling it. It does what he wants it to do. Furthermore, an old brush which is well worn will sometimes become a favorite, for it will create certain lines and effects that are not possible with the perfect new brush. Several old stiff-bristle brushes are good to have around for special effects in foliage and grasses.

Some of the old-school water colorists make a fetish of using a single brush for a whole picture. This brush is a large round No. 12 sable brush, which, with practice, gives striking calligraphic effects. One stroke can make a hair line grow to an inch in width. I use any number of brushes, from four to a dozen, both round and flat. I find a large 1-inch flat brush best for large washes and for clean straight edges. I use a ½-inch brush for smaller areas. A ¼-inch flat brush is fine for creating windows, doors, or any small straight-edged areas. I employ vari-

Stretching water-color paper is important, *very* important. For the best results all papers except the very heavy 300- and 400-pound papers should be stretched. Even for outside work, I recommend stretching a sheet on a board. I have found the following method to be the easiest and safest:

Soak the paper for ten or fifteen minutes in the bathtub, with just enough water to allow the paper to lie flat with both sides wet and with no air pockets between the paper and the water. Then pick up the paper by lifting one side by its two corners; let the water run off the paper until only occasional drops fall from it. Then, still grasping it by the same two corners, hold it at right angles to the drawing board, which is laid flat, and let the bottom edge touch the board; then allow the paper to curve down gently until it lies flat on the dry board. No air bubbles should appear if this is done properly. If there are large air bubbles, lift the paper and try again. If the bubbles persist, the best thing to do is to soak the paper again and for a longer time. Small air bubbles will disappear with the drying of the paper.

For some water colors I wish to have my paper remain wet for a longer period after it is stretched, so I can work on the damp surface. In such cases, I first run water over the side of my drawing board on which the paper is to be stretched, and let the excess water drain off for a few seconds. Then I stretch the paper as described previously and start work soon afterward.

If the paper is soaked for a very long time the surface is destroyed, and the color will not be fresh. Hot water penetrates the paper much more quickly than cold water. It is a good idea for the student to experiment with several small pieces of paper by soaking them for ten minutes, three hours, and twelve hours in both cold and hot water. I have found a full sheet of paper soaked for fifteen minutes stretches nearly half an inch. That explains why it is so very taut after stretching and drying.

The next step is to lay absorbent tissues, such as Kleenex, over the whole surface of the wet paper. Gently pat the tissues, picking up all excess water. A large, clean, white cloth, such as a piece of an old sheet, also serves well. Next, tear off four strips of gummed tape, the kind used for wrapping packages, two inches longer than the sides of the paper. Holding the tape at both ends, run it quickly through a wide, deep dish of water. Snap off the excess water and lay the tape over ½- to ¾-inch of the edge of the paper and the remainder over the board, making sure that it is pressed tightly so that the glue adheres everywhere to both the paper and the board. Occasionally, as the paper dries and contracts, the pull is so strong that the glue comes loose. The odds are that either the paper or the glue tape was too wet. Sometimes the tape tears. If this happens, or if the 2-inch tape will not hold, get a stronger 3-inch tape.

After finishing a water color, I let it dry thoroughly from twelve to twenty-four hours. Then, with a razor blade, I cut through the tape and the outer edge of the paper. The paper should not be cut off before it is dry because it will wrinkle and buckle, making it difficult to handle in matting and framing.

Handle your fine water-color paper with care, especially when it is wet. The wet surface can be easily bruised by a fingernail or knuckle, and later on wet color may flow into the dent and cause a minor disaster.

I have heard that some of the so-called handmade papers have been machine-made in recent years. I am inclined to believe this, for I find, along with other water colorists, that many fine papers made today do not take a wash as well as they once did. I have had difficulty trying to lay large even washes on damp paper; they have often dried with a mottled or streaked appearance. So, although I used to like working on a damp paper, today I find a dry surface more reliable for large flat washes. Also, the bone dry paper gives a fresher and more transparent wash.

Wet paper can also be stretched *over* the sides of a drawing board or canvas stretcher. I find it troublesome, but this is the way to do it if you want to try. Cut out four ¾-inch squares from the four corners of your paper and crease the four sides, ¾ inch from the edge. Then wet the paper in the bathtub and lay the paper over the board as described before. Starting at the middle of each side, and working to the corners while the paper is still moist enough to maneuver easily, carefully tack down the edges with thumbtacks, placing the tacks about 2 inches apart.

DRAWING BOARDS

Drawing boards come in regulation sizes. For most purposes, 20- by 26-inch and 23- by 31-inch boards should serve. I have more than a dozen such boards, so that I can work on a series of water colors and finish them when I feel up to it. Good boards can be made from plywood and Masonite. Large pieces of these materials, say 4 by 8 feet, can be bought from a lumberyard, and the lumber man will cut them into the sizes desired. These may be less expensive than ready-made boards.

19

WORK TABLE

A work table should be large enough to hold your board flat or at an angle and to hold your palette, colors, and water jar without crowding. Be sure that the table is high enough so that you can stand comfortably without bending over too much. The light should come from the side opposite your working hand, to avoid disturbing shadows. See Fig. 1.

GUMMED TAPE

Gummed tape is available in various widths. One- to 2-inch widths are good for stretching small water-color papers on a board. For 15- by 20-inch paper I would use 2-inch tape; for the 20- by 30-inch size use a 2- or 3-inch tape. Rolls of this gummed tape may be purchased in stationery stores. Be sure to get the best quality.

WATER JARS

I recommend two one- or two-quart jars with large openings. For outdoor work, Mason jars which can be sealed tight are fine. You might like an extra jar to hold your brushes.

ABSORBENT TISSUES

I rely on absorbent tissues, such as Kleenex, for purposes as varied as cleaning palettes, brushes, and my hands, to lifting the color out of washes when creating foliage or clouds, as described on page 54. See Figs. 9a and 9b.

SPONGE

A small, soft sponge of the best quality is a wise thing to have by you. It can serve many of the same purposes as the tissues. A sponge is especially good for washing out areas of color and, if there is no bathtub handy, for dampening the paper.

ERASERS

Art gum is the best for erasing pencil lines. You will also need a regular pencil and ink eraser for lightening areas which are too dark. For special uses of erasers and razor blades, see page 57 and Fig. 11.

20

Fig. 1. Work table.

RAZOR BLADES

You will need razor blades for the experiment suggested on page 57; for scraped, mottled effects on dry washes; for ragged effects on wet washes; and for picking out highlights. See Figs. 10 and 11. Buy blades with a single sharp edge, such as Gem blades, so they can be held firmly without danger of cutting the fingers.

ETCHING NEEDLE

An etching needle, or any sharp-pointed instrument, can be used at times instead of the corner of the razor blade, to create similar effects. The handle makes the needle easier to use, and the lines and spots made with the needle will usually be smaller than those made with a razor blade. Special effects with the etching needle are described on page 60 and illustrated in Fig. 14.

SANDPAPER

Sandpaper can be used occasionally for certain purposes. For instance, a coarse piece of sandpaper pulled down over a wet cloud wash can give a fine rain effect. The odds are that you will make a mess out of the first one or two tries, so allow yourself time to experiment. Interesting results can also be attained by sanding over dry washes.

INK

Some purists would not think of using ink, but among the water colorists I know, most of them use ink whenever they feel so inclined. So ink in black and sepia, at least, should be part of your standard equipment. A blacker black can be made with ink than with watercolor. I have used both Higgins and Artone, extra dense. The latter gives a rich black and resists washes that are applied over it. Add a few experiments with ink to those given in the next chapter on black and white exercises. Effects you can achieve by using washes in conjunction with pen lines are demonstrated in Fig. 13.

If you like drawing with pen and ink there is a special artist's fountain pen, Waterman No. 751, which holds black drawing inks. Many artists will not be without one.

RUBBER CEMENT

Apart from its normal use as an adhesive, rubber cement can be valuable in the following way. If you desire clean white areas, particularly small ones, say of birds, clouds, or trees against an evenly washed sky, these small areas can first be painted in with rubber cement. The cement dries quickly, allowing a wash to be applied right over it. After the wash dries, erase the rubber cement by simply rubbing it off with the fingers or with art gum, allowing the white areas to show. With a small brush, light color can then be painted on all or part of these white areas, and a transparency can be attained which would not be possible by trying to paint directly over the wash.

WAX CRAYONS

Wax crayons are useful, and can be used instead of rubber cement to cover an area. The crayon can be scraped off with a razor blade after the washes have dried, but effects are apt to be dirty. There is another use for the crayon which I occasionally employ. When I have a dark area that seems dead, a discreet use of crayon pulled over this surface can liven it up. For instance, a yellow or green crayon over a heavy blue will make it sparkle. Try this trick, but don't overdo it.

A lithographic crayon can also be used. If you want a deeper black than you can get in water color, rub the paper hard with the crayon and a shiny black will sing out. If you plan to use the litho crayon at all, you had better figure on using it from the start; use it to sketch in your composition, creating your shiny blacks, then add your water color. This way the crayon becomes an intrinsic part of your technique. If the picture stands against the wall for several years, the litho crayon will catch dust and the shiny blacks will appear dull and gray. However, you can bring back the shiny blacks by rubbing the surface before you put the picture behind glass and into a frame.

black and white exercises

IT IS QUITE NATURAL FOR YOU TO WANT TO PAINT A PICTURE—A MASTERPIECE—RIGHT away! And I think it is a good idea for you to go ahead and make a try on your own. You may then be ready to check up on a few "do's" and "don't's," unless, of course, you are the perfect primitive. I have a deep sympathy for this feeling of "going it alone," for it was twenty years before I had the courage to stop and learn how to paint a good water color. And then I taught myself. I hope this book may do the same for you—lead you through some interesting experiments and enable you to become your own teacher.

The idea of exercises in water-color technique may sound dull and old-fashioned. Intelligently undertaken, they prove to be neither. Better to enjoy walking before you run, for too many early falls may discourage you from trying again. Give yourself a proper chance by first knowing how to use your tools to the best advantage. You must know how to lay a wash, how to create textures as you need them, how to mix colors, how wet colors blend into each other, and how to glaze one color over another. As you go along you will find endless excitement in observing the results of each step you take, in the variety and beauty that comes out of putting a little color and water onto a piece of white paper.

As one learns to paint by doing and thinking, and not merely by reading, let's get down to a few practical experiments. The following exercises can be done quickly, and the skill and understanding gained from them will help solve the problems which may arise in painting a picture later on.

A water color painted in black is just as much a water color as one employing all the colors of the rainbow. It has always proved to be the best way of starting. Get ready a tube of lampblack or ivory black, a round brush, a flat 1-inch brush, a glass of water, and sheets of drawing paper at least 9 by 12 inches in size. The first three exercises are to be done on dry paper.

24

Fig. 2. Water-color washes from lightest gray to black.

Exercise 1.

Touch your *round* water-color brush, full of water, to the black pigment on your palette; see how light a tint you can make with a single gentle stroke on the dry paper. Add a little more black and use a shade less water for the next brush stroke, placed below the first one. Continue in this way, making as many separate tints of black as you can. You should have nine or ten before you have finished, as shown in Fig. 2.

Exercise 2.

Take your 1-inch *flat* brush and mix a puddle of black, using very little water. With the brush full of this rich black, pull a stroke across the top of your paper. Very quickly touching the brush to water, place another stroke into the lower edge of the first black stroke. Adding more water each time, continue to make parallel strokes, each one touching the bottom of the previous one, down the sheet, until at the bottom of the paper you have the lightest possible tint. At first, the edges of these brush strokes may show. Repeat the exercise often enough so that you can

Fig. 3. A continuous wash from very light to very dark.

gauge the amount of water necessary to attain continuous wash in succeeding strokes from black to the lightest tint, as shown in Fig. 3.

Exercise 3.

You may find it easier to lay a graduated wash if you reverse the foregoing process by starting with the lightest tint and adding the black gradually until you attain the pure black at the bottom of your paper. With enough water in the washes you can tip the board at an angle and the washes will merge easily. This is a neat trick, and you will enjoy doing it. Some flashy water colorists indulge themselves a little too much with this trick; they have been nicknamed the "ebb and flow boys." Used in moderation, the technique is fine. See Fig. 4.

Exercise 4.

After soaking a paper for a short time in water, as described on page 18, lay it on your board, leaving the excess water on the paper. Try making washes and lines with a brush on this flooded surface. It blurs beyond all control, so learn this. Too wet is too wet and is no good unless you particularly plan a blurred, overall fuzzy effect. In this case, apply color to the flooded paper, let it dry, then work

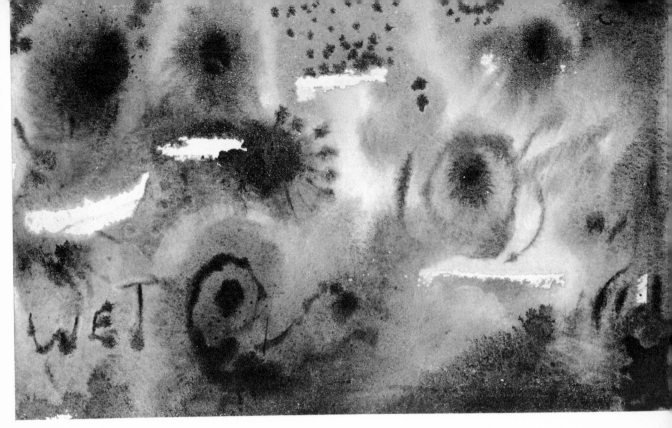

Fig. 4. "Ebb and flow" experiments, with darker washes laid over a wet base wash.

over it with stronger and sharper brush strokes. Some interesting results can be achieved this way.

Exercise 5.

Again soak a paper, then mop up all excess water with absorbent tissues. Now lay on washes as you did in Exercises 1, 2, and 3. You will discover you can lay washes more leisurely on the damp paper and that they will blend more easily. However, if you compare these washes you made on dry paper, you will see that the wash on dry paper tends to have greater freshness and clarity.

By this time you should have a working knowledge of laying washes on dry and wet papers.

Exercise 6.

Take a small round brush full of pigment, without water, and draw lines into a good-sized wash of gray which is still wet. Interesting fuzzy lines emerge, the degree of fuzziness depending upon the wetness of the paper. Put more lines down as the wash dries, and see how much less fuzzy they are. Finally, draw into the dried wash and observe how hard and sharp the line becomes. See Fig. 5.

Next, take the same brush, mix the black with water to get a dark gray, and draw it into another wash which is still wet. Also mix lighter grays (which means having more water in your brush) and draw into the same wash. Notice how they will blur and merge with the wet washes. If the wash is very wet, the edge of the stroke marks will disappear altogether. Later, when the wash is dry, the same brush with the same gray washes will give clean crisp lines.

This is stressed so that you will realize what happens when using paper of various degrees of wetness. Soon you will know how to coordinate the amount of pigment and water in the brush and the degree of wetness and dryness of the washes to get the effects you want. Timing becomes an important factor in water-color painting. When you know it so well that your hand *feels* it, you are surely on the high road to being a water colorist.

Exercise 7.

The dry brush technique allows for a great range of textures. I have seen large, complex water colors done this way. Take a good-sized brush full of black pigment and brush it out on your paper until the brush is so dry that only the high points of the grain of the paper catch the color. Continued gentle rubbing with the brush will make more delicate tones. The granular effect will depend on the grain of paper. If coarse grain effects are desired, a rough paper *must* be used. This rubbing is hard on the brushes, and I recommend using old or poor brushes for this activity. Dark tones can be rubbed over lighter washes effectively after the latter have dried. These results are useful when your washes get dull; they will liven up areas, especially in foliage and grasses.

Exercise 8.

Scrubbing washes. Take an old large brush full of water and scrub into a dried wash. As you continue scrubbing to and fro the pigment picks up. Continued scrubbing will bring the paper back to white, but it will also destroy the sizing in the paper. Later washes over these soft, scrubbed areas will lack the sparkle of those done on the original sized surface. A sponge is fine for scrubbing larger surfaces. Occasionally, when a water color has gone haywire or, let's say, a sky I have done has "run away from me," I have placed that part of the board to be washed in five or six inches of water (in the bathtub) and scrubbed it with a large, clean, white rag until all pigment has gone. Sometimes after brief wetting and slight scrubbing certain parts of the color that sank into the paper more deeply will remain, suggesting possibilities of redeveloping. Some most depressing efforts have,

Fig. 5. The whole area was covered with a light, uneven wash. After it dried, lighter and darker washes were laid over it, giving clean edges.

in this manner, been transformed into successful paintings. Every artist learns that some mistakes can turn out to be happy ones if he is constantly on the lookout for new and interesting effects. So, when doing these exercises, always be aware of the possibilities presented by a partially scrubbed wash; it may present an attractive texture that you could not get any other way.

Take a small brush, dip it in water, and pull it easily over a dry gray wash. Nothing happens. Pull it over the same stroke twenty or more times and notice that gradually a light line appears. If this is done carefully, the edges can be quite clean. The effect you get with this technique is often useful.

Next, try your skill by washing a square inch out of a dry gray wash to make it a lighter gray or white. Try this several times and see how sharp and clean an edge you can make.

These exercises are valuable; even practicing artists continually experiment in this sort of way to improve certain techniques. Don't underestimate their importance. They will get you thoroughly acquainted with the tools and materials at your disposal. It is a good idea to keep your exercise sheets for future reference. You can borrow this, that, or the other effect when you start painting a picture in earnest—using more colors.

exercises for painting in color

Now you will want to get going with color. So before any new exercises are suggested, why not a preliminary spree? Put little globs of all your colors on the palette and let yourself go. On several different sheets of not-too-valuable paper make color doodles; make lines and washes of all colors and let them flow into each other until you are weary. Having now tasted blood; having experienced the emotional satisfaction of using color; in fact, having now had an unrestrained fling, you may feel ready to take another clean sheet and once more bring a little order out of chaos.

Previously we worked with black. Let us continue this study a little further by learning the difference between lampblack and ivory black—how cold and blue the former, how warm and brown the latter. In all future painting it is important to remember this difference, in using the color either alone or in relation to other colors. You should experiment with black inks, too, and note their effects.

There are also colors such as Payne's gray, charcoal gray, and neutral tint, which, when used in full intensity, make near blacks. Notice the cold bluish tints made with Payne's gray, the lavender aspect of neutral tint, and how charcoal gray comes closer to the ivory.

Today artists have almost entirely overcome the prejudice against using black in water-color painting—and high time. Renoir avoided black for ten years and then, going back to it, said, "Black is the queen of colors." I would rather say, at least in water-color painting, "Black is the king of colors and white paper is the queen." Purists argue that using black is an easy and sneaky way to get neutral tones. They also point to the lack of brilliance and luminosity. This is true to some extent. But the pure black or gray tint, unmixed with any other color, can set off and enhance the beauty of all other colors. Sometimes I choose to mix

30

black or one of the three grays mentioned above with other colors to neutralize them. I purposely choose not to have all the brilliance in a gray that might be obtained by mixing together other colors. These dull or dead grays can, by contrast, make the bright colors in a water color more brilliant. There is, of course, always the danger that you may overdo the use of blacks and grays, relying on them to get all your neutral tones and grays. Payne's gray can become especially pernicious in this respect, so watch out.

If you have made an extensive study of contemporary painting, you may agree that black—as Roualt and so many artists since have used it—to outline nearly everything, has been considerably overworked. It is an easy way to pull color and composition together. By all means do it if you see fit, but don't get into the habit of relying on it all the time when you get to the point of picture making.

It is now necessary to become intimately acquainted with the character of all the other colors. As in the experiments with black, take each color separately and make the most delicate washes, then more washes of various intensities until the color is used to its full strength. Then paint darker strokes into the lighter washes. Observe how much darker the color is while it is still wet. As it dries, it will become lighter. Always remember this in future painting. A water color often looks exciting and full of contrasts when wet, only to seem dull and anemic by comparison when it has dried.

To get the brightest possible color you may use less pigment and more water, instead of using it thick and pure out of the tube. Observe how blackish alizarin crimson looks when you apply it just as it comes out of the tube, how brilliant it is when mixed with a little water, and then how it peters out into delicate cold, pinkish tints when mixed with a lot of water.

Certain colors, such as Naples yellow, Payne's gray, vermilion, cobalt and cerulean blue and chromium oxide dull green, are more opaque and the pigment tends to lie on the surface of the paper. Other colors, such as Hooker's green, Prussian blue and alizarin red, penetrate into the paper and are hard to scrub off.

The main things to observe and store away in your memory are the character of each color as it stands alone in relationship to the paper and how the paper changes the character of the color as more water is added. The water colorist must comprehend this fully to be successful. Vermilion is a good color as an example. Make various tints, from the pure color out of the tube to the most delicate tint. Notice that the hot, pure vermilion, as it gets lighter, becomes cooler and pinker. The character of the light pink has little of its original color left. This means the white paper becomes part of the color. So you must know that the more water used with the color the lighter and cooler the tone. This is what makes the water color different from all oil or other opaque painting. The artist is always considering, at least indirectly, the paper as an element along with the color and that is one reason at least why many oil painters say they cannot paint water colors.

COMBINING COLORS

1. Vermilion Red, Alizarin Crimson, Indian Red (or Venetian Red)

Make washes of these colors separately and of various intensities, and then let one liquid wash merge with another. Paint darker, smaller washes, lines, and dots into these wet washes as they dry, and after they are dry. You will be surprised at the range you can get from these three reds. See how a tint of alizarin red sparkles and how opaque a dark shade of Indian red will be when painted over it. Make a composition of these three colors, leaving some white paper, and see how effective it is.

2. Sepia, Burnt Sienna (or Burnt Umber)

Repeat the foregoing with these colors. Then make a composition with one of these two colors, and in another composition add black. Handsome water colors or wash drawings have always been made with shades of browns and blacks, and you may find you like using a monochromatic color scheme. Do not be afraid to use the pure color as it comes from the tube, with no water, or very little water, to get intense darks and powerful accents.

When buying tube colors you will find that there are two sepias—sepia and warm sepia. Warm sepia is lighter, browner, warmer; and you may prefer this. I have them both on hand. In the same way there are even greater differences in the siennas and umbers. Try them out and make a note of your preferences.

3. Cadmium Yellow, Lemon Yellow, Naples Yellow, Yellow Ocher

Repeat the exercises you have already done with the blacks, reds, and browns. These three yellows give a startling range. The daintiness of a lemon yellow tint is scarcely discernible on the white paper, quite different from the sharp brashness of a bright cadmium yellow deep or the dull, opaque, pastel quality of Naples yellow. But these differences are what give the great range, variety, and body to your color composition. Observe how weak even a strong tint of yellow is against the white paper. Surround it with a dark color, like sepia, and it becomes brilliant. After this experiment you will be increasingly aware of one of the great principles in art: that a color standing alone (or against white) has one aspect, but when related to other colors and values it will take on quite another character. For in-

32

stance, a neutral green surrounded by bright yellows will hardly seem green at all, but rather bluish. Surrounded by deep blues, the same neutral green will look warm and green.

Mix your black pigment with the different yellows and you will have variations of a somber olive green which, standing alone, may or may not please you, but which, in your battle to get a range of greens in a summer landscape, for instance, will be extremely useful. Actually I love the olive greens, particularly the shades made with cadmium yellow and the blacks, and I use this combination often. You will find Naples yellow very opaque; and when mixed with black it produces a bluish gray tone, rather dusty and milky, which in itself is unsympathetic, but again has its place in relation to other colors. I once used it successfully in painting a Western dust storm.

Little globs of Naples yellow lifted right out of the tube with the brush and placed onto a drying dark area can enliven the dark area with unexpected textural effects.

4. Cobalt Blue, Ultramarine, Prussian Blue

These three blues can be varied by substituting any one of the following: cerulean blue, Winsor new blue, and monastral blue. Generally I do not use more than two blues in one picture, however there can be no rule about this. Try out cobalt, ultramarine, and Prussian blue, first; later experiment with the others in varying shades and combinations.

Be sparing in the use of powerful pigments such as Prussian and monastral blue. Many water colorists overdo these. They are so strong that they kill the subtleties of the other colors, particularly in landscapes where a shrieking blue sky can ruin an otherwise quite satisfactory color arrangement.

Prussian blue and yellow ocher or burnt umber will make dark and exciting greens. Prussian blue, black, and opaque white make a fine gray. Cerulean blue and Naples yellow give an unusual green which I occasionally enjoy using.

5. Chromium Oxide Dull Green, Hooker's Green No. 2 (extra dark), Emerald Green, Permanent Green Pale (May Green), Olive Green

Repeat the same exercises as before, using these greens. Notice the full-bodied opacity of a thick wash of chromium oxide dull green and the transparency of a delicate tint of the same color. To get a brilliant sky I have quite often used a thin wash of this color. The Hooker's green is powerful, poisonous, and dangerous, but useful for certain effects. Observe the bluish tints of the lightest tones on the white paper, and lift the color onto the brush without water to see what an unbelievable black green it makes. With a brushful of this color you can scumble black-green textures over lighter greens and make excellent foliage textures. Remember to try this before you give up a foliage painting as lost.

Emerald green is considered permanent if not mixed with other colors. The temptation to use emerald green and May green is great, for they have unequaled freshness; but don't overdo it.

Remember the other greens you can mix yourself from black and yellow and blue and yellow, as suggested previously. Many artists never use a tube green— they mix their own; but this is really a question of individual preference.

6. Opaque White (Chinese White)

Opaque white is both fascinating and dangerous for the water colorist. Purists object to a mixture of white with other colors, claiming that it kills brilliancy and transparency. They are right in this, of course, but the evil can also be a virtue. Many water-color paintings are thin and superficial. One reason for this is that their perpetrators are so bent on transparency, luminosity, and the beautiful flow of one color tint into another, that they forget about the texture and body of objects. Often their rocks and mountains are too cloudy, their clouds too rocky. Mountains obviously must have more solidity than the fluffy clouds floating airily above them.

Semiopaque and even real opaque tones will help give body and texture. How much more a transparent sky appears like a sky when the foreground of the painting has been given a solid feeling of earth, rocks and vegetation.

I find myself simultaneously recommending and warning against opaque whites. Use white, or use it mixed with another color to make that color opaque; but use it *sparingly,* and at least refrain from using it until the picture is already well developed. The odds are you will run into several dead ends before you learn to control it. If you do overdo the use of white, remember that the bath treatment may yet save the day. Opaque white, or colors mixed with white, will, for the most part, lie on the surface of the paper. If you put the water color into the bathtub some of the opaque colors will flood off quite easily, and it may be that you will find new and unexpected color arrangements, making you eager to resume the painting on a different tack.

Make three little square washes of opaque white—one as the thick moist white comes from the tube, the second a medium mixture of white with water, and the third a light tint of the white. When these have dried, compare the three closely; also compare them with the surrounding paper. They will appear dull or dead by comparison with the paper, which is a more brilliant white. This simple experiment is important in demonstrating how to get both warm and cold whites with different textures.

Mix various washes using little white and much white with the different colors of your palette. See how chalky and dull they are in comparison with the fresh washes of pure transparent colors, and how, at the same time, they have more body. Mix white and black and notice the interesting grays. Glaze a thin, watery wash of white over dried washes and see what dusty, milky effects appear. Remember how each of your successful experiments was done, for later use. Some people find it helpful to make notes on their worksheets describing exactly how a particularly successful or unusual effect was achieved.

THE PRIMARY COLORS

Red, yellow, and *blue* are, of course, the three primary colors from which all other colors stem, except for pure black and pure white.

THE SECONDARY COLORS

Orange, green, and *violet* are the secondary colors; each is the result of combining two primary colors.

Orange is made by mixing red and yellow. Mix different intensities of wash made with lemon yellow and vermilion. Do the same with cadmium yellow and alizarin. Repeat with yellow ocher and Indian red. Then try combinations of the three yellows and three reds. You should have many oranges to wonder at and admire.

Green is made by mixing yellow and blue. Just as you mixed all the yellows and reds, combine the yellows and blues and see the fine assortment of greens that come out of your brush. Remember, or note down, which combinations give you the best greens, so you can repeat them later.

Violet is made by combining blue and red. You should find some tender lilacs and sonorous purples which may give you a sensuous thrill. But use them with caution.

THE TERTIARY COLORS

Citron, russet, and *olive* are the tertiary colors; each is the result of combining two secondary colors.

Citron is made with orange and green; russet is made with orange and violet; olive is made with violet and green.

Experiment with the various oranges, greens, and violets and watch the citrons, russets, and olives appear. Note that as more colors are mixed together the original brilliance peters out and they become more grayed and neutral.

COMPLEMENTARY COLORS

By mixing two primary colors, the secondary color is produced. This color is the complementary of the remaining primary. For example:

Red and yellow make orange, the complementary of blue.
Red and blue make purple, the complementary of yellow.
Yellow and blue make green, the complementary of red.

Now mix the various complementary colors with each other and note how they neutralize each other, producing warm or cool grays.

WARM AND COLD COLOR

Colors are either warm or cold, and the degree varies. *Warm colors are yellow, orange, and red. Cold colors are violet, blue, and green.*

Lemon yellow is cooler than cadmium yellow, so we speak of hot and cold yellows. The same is true of red; a vermilion leaning toward orange is hot; an alizarin leaning toward purple is cool. A yellow green is warmer than a blue green. The blues are all cool, but even there we find green blue warmer than an intense Prussian blue. Ivory black is warmer than lampblack. There are warm and cool grays, depending on whether they are yellowish (warmer) or bluish (cooler). The same is true of whites. One speaks of a warm white paper if its tone is yellowish, a cold white paper if the tone is bluish.

VALUE

Each color has value. The value of the colors fit between the lightest shade to black like this: *yellow, very light; orange, light; red and green, light medium to dark; blue, dark; violet, very dark.* From this you can see that the warm colors are generally of a lighter value, the cool ones of a dark value.

In painting, the awareness of the value of each color is of utmost importance. In fact, the power and effect of each color depends upon its value as much as it depends upon its intensity. For example, here is what could happen if the value of color was ignored. Visualize a light yellow-green tree against a light sky of a different color but of exactly the same value. It would not show up enough; and the picture, spatially and compositionally, would be ruined. If the color value of the tree were deepened several shades, the effect would be entirely different.

painting in water color

By now you should feel that you have a pretty good working knowledge of your tools. The brush feels familiar in your hand, you know how to lay washes, you have observed the very important relationship of paper to color, and you know how to mix colors.

It may be that you feel you should have a greater knowledge about the theory of color. There is really only one way you can come to understand color. Work with it. Learn through practice, through trial and error, through observing nature and studying the works of the artists you most admire. Original, distinguished color comes out of the individual, based on his observations, experiences, and spontaneous reactions. Balance your color as nature does; play light against dark and dark against light; place bright colors in smaller quantities against larger areas of subdued or neutral colors. Look for highlights, and plan accents of color that vibrate and bring the picture alive. If there is any rule to follow, it is to avoid unnatural colors and contrived effects.

In starting to paint, make small compositions of anything that appeals to you —landscapes, figures, and pure abstractions. For those with less experience in draftsmanship, it is a fine idea to learn to think in abstract terms; but whatever you do, don't regard the first fumblings and doodlings as great works of art. Give yourself time.

There are two reasons why it is good for the student to paint abstractly. First, the design of any picture is right only if the abstract shapes have balance and rhythm. It is useful to experiment with this in mind. Whatever literal connotations a painting may carry will be of secondary importance in such experiments. Secondly, by working abstractly the student will be free of notions of local color (a tree is green, a sky is blue, etc.). He will more easily dare to combine any and

37

all colors into unique relationships, and he should come upon exciting and startling ones. These experiments can be a creative starting point for a more literal picture later on—unless, of course, you become wedded to the abstract style of painting for keeps.

You may find a certain passage of color turns out beautifully, yet does not relate to the finished design as a whole. Always, always, have the courage to sacrifice the detail for the whole. One can say that this is really a rule, and for all types of painting.

At first you will be wise to limit your palette to five or six colors. The chances are that you will learn more rapidly this way, for it is less bewildering. As a start, why not try yellow ocher, cadmium yellow, vermilion, Indian red, monastral blue, and emerald green. Don't forget that large, cool areas of color are effectively relieved by bringing in some warm color, such as a red barn against a blue-green sky—to take a literal example. The reverse would be equally true; a blue-green barn against a red sky.

The beginner nearly always wants to do too much. Try to be strong-willed and hold back. Choose a simple subject and try to think of the masses of light and dark and the masses of color. Forget all detail in the beginning; start worrying about it only when the picture nears completion. Remember also that the overall composition is most important. Eliminate all extraneous objects. You are creating a picture, not duplicating nature exactly, as in a photograph. Do not be afraid of ignoring the actual color you see before you, if you have the inclination to create a different mood. You will, of course, realize that it will be necessary to simplify the nuances of color that you see in nature, even if you should wish to copy them exactly.

Do try to go beyond a too-literal interpretation. You should try to put down not what you *see*, so much as what you *feel*. If that is done, your picture is on the way to being a success. If this feeling of yours is intense, and if your statement is true and not a copy of the other fellow, your painting is on the way to being an important work of art. If you fail the first time, don't be discouraged. Keep on trying. There are plenty more sheets of paper.

Now there is always someone around who will say, "I don't want to paint what I feel, I only want to paint what I see." Though we will grant that his problem might be one of semantics, he has every right to talk and do as he chooses. Everyone has to approach the problem of painting in his on particular way. And he goes through numerous phases. Finally, however, imagination scores as high as technique—or where do you think Picasso would be?

The nature of water-color painting is such that when a picture is developed to a certain point it is either good, not so good, or bad. Don't stew over an indifferent picture. If the subject is interesting to you, set up the picture and do another one from it, benefiting from your mistakes. Many times I make several versions of a subject before I get what I really want. Although the water colorist should have speed and dexterity and sail through a sky like a bird, he must also be prepared to be as patient and plodding as a mole!

There are some demons of the brush who turn out four or five water colors in an afternoon and who count on picking out the lucky accident as his *pièce de résistance*. I have read such an "expert's" statement that "no water color should take more than an hour to make." Don't be taken in. It does not matter whether you take thirty minutes or thirty weeks to complete a water color. I have made little sketches in less than thirty minutes, but the average large water color will take anywhere from several hours to a week. Charles Burchfield told me that he once had in his studio a very large water color which he worked on from time to time for seven years.

It is a fine idea to set up earlier works and study them. Often you will see what needs to be done and you can make improvements. Time lends a fresh eye and objectivity. Save all your sketches, try-outs, and masterpieces; let time decide which eventually should be discarded and which should be framed.

During the early stages you may often become discouraged and feel unable to cope with color; or you may think that you cannot dream up any more original themes and schemes. I assure you that this phenomena persists through the years. On and off, most practicing artists face just the same problem. Take the day off, do something quite different, or concentrate on drawing. No artist has ever done too much of this! Or go back to doodling with all colors. Mix them without thinking. An hour of this activity has often set me off to work with new eagerness. Set up a good reproduction of some masterpiece you particularly admire and copy it. Copy it literally or adapt it freely, as you wish. You can learn much about composition and how other artists put colors together. Don't worry about losing your personality by copying. You won't lose it this way unless you make a regular practice of it. Try everything from Homer to Marin or from Sargeant to Burchfield and keep going back to your way of thinking, watching how your own style progresses.

composition

THE CLASSIC RULES ABOUT COMPOSITION ARE NUMEROUS ENOUGH TO HAVE FILLED several books on the subject, but the few general hints we have room for here may prove helpful to beginners. They should perhaps be prefaced, arbitrarily, by the observation that most contemporary artists say "break all rules on composition as you see fit."

A square sheet of paper divided into two equal parts is not as interesting as one divided into unequal parts. Consequently, artists generally do not put the horizon exactly in the middle of the paper. I have done it often, however, and then tried to break up the sky and earth areas interestingly enough so that the even half and half division was overcome (see Fig. 6*a*). Carrying this rule farther, you will find that an asymmetrical balance of unequal shapes and sizes of objects is more interesting than a whole row of equal ones. Again one will find that a certain amount of equal sizes, heights, and lengths are important to provide a contrast with the unequal ones.

There should be one main object or center of interest, such as a person or group of people, a building, a tree, a boat, or a road, to which all the objects are to a greater or lesser degree subservient. This center of interest should have its greatest area to the left or right of center and either below or above the middle of the picture. It should be balanced by other objects or strong enough areas of color, so that the picture holds together as a unit.

One lonely color is not as thrilling to behold as two or more colors happily juxtaposed. If you use all the colors of the rainbow you may have a gay kaleidoscopic effect; but these colors need organization—one color should dominate, the others accompany. The intensities, values, shapes, and sizes of the color areas should be varied and well balanced. Texture, the play of the hard surface against

Fig. 6a. Cutting the picture plane right in the middle usually makes an even, uninteresting composition. This was done deliberately in this sketch to show how the picture can still be redeemed by breaking up the two equal areas into diverse, smaller shapes.

the soft surface and the tender fuzzy line against the sharp line, contributes much to the pleasant effect of good design.

Plan structural compositional lines right from the beginning. In other words, first indicate the skeleton of your design. Then fit your areas of color masses and details into them. Plan always to make the eye of the beholder flow into the picture from the outside border and dwell on the focal point or center of interest. No lines or colors should carry the eye too violently out of the margins. Don't have too much exciting detail or contrast very near the borders or in the corners. Also, within the inner confines of the picture itself, do not draw too much attention to spots or lines which are secondary to the main theme, or the picture will look "busy." Take simple themes first, then work up to more detailed compositions as you gain in confidence.

41

Fig. 6b. Here the process described in Fig. 6a was reversed. The picture plane was unevenly divided to make an interesting composition, but the details of the landscape are even and monotonous. Observe, also, how the road and tree pull the eye out of the lower left corner of the picture, then again how the road pulls the eye out of the picture in the opposite direction. The sameness of the rolling mountains and cloud formation and the dull spacing of the flat area have nothing of interest to excite the eye.

drawing and perspective

ALTHOUGH THIS BOOK CONCERNS ITSELF WITH TECHNIQUES IN WATER-COLOR, GOUACHE and casein painting, I add this short chapter of suggestions for the beginner who has had no formal training in drawing. Often people say "I love color, it's easy for me to paint with color, but I don't know how to draw. How can I learn?" The following may help.

The only real way to learn to draw is, of course, by drawing, and by doing more and more drawing. In your spare time take a pencil and sketch pad and draw all the things about you, starting with simple objects, such as a cup and a saucer, a box or a sofa. Then put several objects together, arranging them into what seems a good composition. Try to get the correct proportions of the objects. Use the same intelligence in figuring this out that you would use in fixing the engine of your car or sewing your dress.

Drawing people and animals is more fun—and more difficult. One has the added problem of action and character. Figure out the proportions of the various parts of the body to the whole body. The head and neck will go into the full length of the figure from five to six and a half times. See how big the hand is in relation to the face and forearm. Compare all parts to each other. In drawing, the proportions and action should be considered simultaneously. Consider the motion of the whole body and its basic direction, and then consider the special directions taken by arms, legs, neck, and head. It will probably be easiest to do this in small, quick sketches from two to six inches high; you will not be tempted by detail. At first, don't attempt to put in features or other details in these sketches. Let that come later. Observe how the parts of the body fit into each other, arm into shoulder, head and neck into the body, legs into buttocks and pelvis, etc. A thorough knowledge of the construction of the figure makes it possible for the artist to draw

43

Fig. 7. A page from the author's sketch book.

figures in any position. There are many books on anatomy and you may find it helpful to study them—and those on perspective, too.

These give such rules as:

The space between the eyes equals the space of one eye.

The distance between the ears equals the distance between the eyebrows and chin.

The lower lip is midway between the bottom of the nose and the bottom of the chin.

The arm, when bent, will measure twice the head from the top of the shoulder to the elbow, and twice from the elbow to where the four fingers begin on the palm of the hand.

I must repeat that facility in drawing can come only from continued practice. Carry a small sketch book in your pocket; and wherever and whenever you have time to spare, whether in the park, on the street, in a restaurant, make sketches. Sketch a whole landscape, limiting yourself to ten minutes; then sketch the objects in the landscape separately, the trees, houses, rocks, leaves, grasses, skies, the quadrupeds and bipeds, and by all means peds or tripeds if you see any—and if you don't, yet have the impulse, make them up. Which brings up an important point: if you have an impulse toward fantasy, let yourself go. It's a great relaxation and such drawings are just as worth while as the more conventional subjects.

The perspective of three-dimensional objects can be quite a problem. However, even the uninitiated know the perspective lesson of the railroad and telephone poles converging at one point on the horizon—at eye level. Always remember the third dimension of any object, that is, that part of the object which goes away from you, will have all lines above the level of the eye slant downward toward eye level, while all lines below the eye level will travel upward. Sitting in a large room, you can easily observe this. The ceiling lines go downward and the floor lines go upward. That is the essence of perspective, although there are ramifications that only specialists such as architects need understand fully.

The second thing to know about perspective is easy to learn after the above has been understood. A large box placed cater-cornered, that is, with its forward corner facing you at an angle, shows two sides going away from you toward two imaginary points on the horizon line, one to the left, one to the right. In drawing, these imaginary points will probably be outside the confines of your drawing pad. See the perspective drawing, Fig. 8.

Remember also that clouds have perspective. Observe this on a summer day when there are lots of them in the sky. They can be large, above you, and with

Fig. 8. A lesson in perspective.

areas of blue around them, then, as they near the horizon line, they appear small with no blue sky showing. Notice how crisp and clear they are in the upper part of the sky and how much grayer and closer in value they appear in the distance.

In drawing objects, bearing this theory in mind, one can help oneself by relating the direction of all lines that make up the contours and shapes of objects to a plumb line and to the horizontal, which will be at right angles to the plumb line. In fact, many art students use a horizontal or plumb line to draw a perpendicular and help them get the exact direction of converging lines. A plumb line can be made with a piece of cord and anything tied on one end which is weighty enough to hold the cord taut when suspended; usually a small piece of lead is used.

All artists, even academic artists, take certain liberties with perspective for legitimate esthetic reasons. However, one should know how to draw objects in perspective and only then ignore rules—for a well thought out reason.

To get the proportions of distant objects, artists frequently use the simple de-

47

vice of holding a pencil at arm's length between the eye and the object to be measured. The pencil is held by the thumb and forefinger with enough of the pencil above the thumb to measure the object in question; then, still keeping the arm at full length and not moving the thumb, see how many times that measurement fits into the larger objects related to it. Do this with the human figure and see how many times the head and neck will go into the full length of the figure. The answer should average five and a half or six times.

The beginner will find that good hard thinking and observation will reveal most of the necessary knowledge about anatomy, proportion, gesture, and perspective. This activity should never be torture. Actually, it is fascinating. The student's drawing will improve most by observing, then drawing continuously with spontaneity and speed. Not too much time should be spent in getting all proportions exact. Try to get the big proportion, action, and character. Then check up afterward on classic proportions, and profit by mistakes. After a few weeks, and again after a few months, compare these sketches with your earlier ones; there should be an astonishing improvement.

Never give up drawing the things you see and like; many sketches of individual objects can be used in a painting later. And never allow yourself to feel self-conscious with a pencil and pad in your hands. You are out to learn something, and you will. Remember that many great artists were self-taught, and the individual styles of those like Van Gogh are a lasting monument to a man's ingenuity and perseverence.

landscape in water color

MOST PEOPLE WISH TO PAINT LANDSCAPES, AND MOST OF THEM FEEL THIS MUST BE done out of doors. On the face of it, this seems reasonable enough. I must first state why I am an unreasonable iconoclast on this point.

I am lazy; I can't imagine carrying around boxes of paints, drawing boards, sketch books, easels, collapsible stools to sit on and maybe, as some do, an umbrella to ward off the rays of the sun. My preoccupation with paraphernalia would be so great that the poet in me would wilt. I cling to the nation that the landscape painter should have the maximum thrill that Mother Nature can give him. So, unencumbered, I wander over hill and dale, through barbed wire fences, over hay and wheat fields, through farmyards and barns, and when inspiration strikes me, quickly I pull out my sketch book and pencil and draw just enough to capture the necessary shapes and the relationships of hill to rock to sky to barn to tree to house to man to cow to chicken to pig to blade of grass.

This data-sketch, with a few color notes marked in, gives just enough material to start my picture. The sketches, usually without much detail, revive my memory only of the big scene and the prevailing mood. If I want to, I can feel free to re-arrange the whole basic structure, I can create a color scheme which may directly relate to my memory or, as often happens, I find a new scheme growing on its own, one color wash suggesting the one to use next. The spontaneous flow of water color without active planning, just a dashing ahead, can bring forth the very best picture—and sometimes, let's face it, the worst. However skilled an artist may be, an element of luck always enters into the making of a water color.

The outdoor painter, by now weary and sweating under the weight of his equipment, is likely to compromise on the first likely spot and set up his stand for the day. He will soon be captured by a certain mood, enchanted by certain effects of light and shade; then just when he is nicely started, a cloud comes along and that's that. After waiting for the same light to return, he impatiently starts faking from memory, then the cloud goes away and he tries to revert to the original plan. By this time he is also in a state about the flies, mosquitoes, ants; and as the final payoff, a Philistine wanders by to admire or criticize.

Confronted by the endless details of nature outdoors, every blade of grass claiming attention, every nuance of color and line so rich and alluring, I find it hard to simplify details sufficiently to get the big design that I know is most important.

There is yet another fact to take into account: the finished painting will hang indoors. Your picture may look well in bright daylight, but in subdued indoor light, or under artificial light, the colors may let you down. Outdoor painters tell me they learn to select colors with this in mind, but I doubt that there is any foolproof method.

My strongest argument for painting indoors is that the artist has a better chance of putting his imagination to work when he paints in the studio. He recalls the most important elements of an outdoor scene and can simplify and rearrange the structure and color of his sketch into a more direct and exciting design. He can play up the more interesting features and play down or eliminate any details that may confuse the organization of the picture into a dramatic whole. No artist ever thinks he can improve on nature. He knows he can't. Some, however, do their best to imitate it; while others, knowing that photography can do a better "literal" job, use their ingenuity in bringing out the feeling or mood that their subject suggests—they try, for example, to capture the living essence of a tree, rather than to represent the minute details of every leaf. Lines and shapes may be exaggerated, colors may be heightened, cloud formations may be introduced into a landscape for the sole purpose of making a picture alive and moving and different from a photograph. The artist has to be a poet as well as a recorder, and he usually has more time to be one in the studio.

The quick diagrammatic pencil sketches, made outdoors, are all that I, personally, need to stimulate my memory. I find a highly detailed drawing not so good, for I am tempted to put it all into my water color, making it more static or too "busy" with detail. My outdoor sketch may take as little as five or ten minutes, or it may take an hour. I use a 2B pencil, which is quite soft but does not smudge too easily. Sometimes I use a lithographic crayon or pen and ink. Almost any sketch book is all right. I use various sizes, from the small ones that can be carried in my pocket to those measuring up to 15 by 20 inches. The smoother surfaces are more agreeable for pencil, as well as for pen and ink.

I write into the sketch book any data about color which may help my memory, but usually I find that I ignore the literal color notes unless I have a commission to paint a special place. In this case I draw the scene with much more detail and get my proportions and the color notes quite correct, for the painting is really to be a portrait, not an interpretation of nature in a general sense. Objects that are difficult and detailed in construction and perspective are worked out carefully, whereas skies, fields, hills and trees may be indicated with a line or two, with notes on color and texture. Obviously, if the owner of the place who commissioned such a work finds the painter has taken too many artistic liberties—has painted the house with red shutters instead of blue, or has lopped off that new wing, eliminated the tool shed, or planted a few more trees in the garden—he is going to send the picture right back where it came from.

Having said all this, I may at first seem to be contradicting myself when I recommend that the beginner *should* paint out of doors. Everyone must have this experience. Do a lot of it at the start; but whenever your painting fails, set the painting up indoors and do it over. Also try starting a picture outdoors and finishing it indoors. As time goes on and you have a backlog of experience with the forms of nature, with color relationships, and with your medium, you may wish to work in the studio more and more often. This has been the trend among contemporary artists for a long time. Each individual is different, and only by trying out everything can he determine which practice is best suited to his own particular makeup and talents. In any event, you must go out of doors to make sketches and color notes from nature, even if you don't make your whole painting under the skies.

The following are some suggestions which I think may help the student with his first efforts at landscape painting:

A simple wash, lighter and warmer at the horizon line, blending into darker and cooler shades toward the top, can be the basis for the sky. That may be all you need. However, you can also work darker shades into such a sky while it is still wet or damp, using a smaller brush. These washes should merge with the original wash, giving soft edges characteristic of clouds. When the washes are dry you can lay on tints. These will be very sharp and crisp. If, however, immediately after laying the tint, a portion of it is lifted with absorbent tissues, the effect can become very delicate. (Notes on special cloud effects obtained by the use of absorbent tissues will be found on page 54.)

Be careful of deep blues. No sky is very intense or blue if you compare it with the really deep, intense colors found in the earth below. I have often observed when sitting on juries of large water color exhibitions that many paintings were ruined by dark blues such as Prussian and monastral. Many artists avoid painting a blue sky altogether.

I have had fair luck by mixing cerulean blue, a little chromium oxide dull green or May green, and a touch of opaque white to get a well-behaved sky, also new blue, white, or Naples yellow and a touch of black. Always remember that any color is good only as it relates to the rest of the design.

LANDSCAPE GREENS

We now come to the problem of the greens of the earth in summertime, when most landscapes are painted. Green, the most soothing of colors, optical experts tell us, has driven more than one landscape artist to the deserts of New Mexico. Another fine way to avoid green is to paint in the autumn, winter, or in very early spring when green is a tender yellow-green, not a strident ubiquitous harridan as she is in summer. However, if we take a good look at Courbet's landscapes, we find that green is not impossible to paint and we can, in fact, must, try it. Dare to be arbitrary; take liberties, if need be, with the greens you see; exaggerate them, understate them, do anything you can think of to get a nice play of greens. Again remember that the other colors you use with the greens can make or break them. Try black with yellow, umber and reds with greens from the tube, ochers with blues. This will give you a pretty good range of greens. Don't try to make all bright greens, for in nature they are not as bright as you may be tempted to believe.

Observe how the sun during the middle of the day saps the color out of nature. As the afternoon advances, the colors are again more exciting. For this reason, many artists prefer not to work out of doors during the noon hours.

When painting outdoors it is easy to be baffled by the detail and range of color. We know that a meadow is green, but we see light and shadow creating variations of green. How to relate all this to the greens on our palette? Observe that the different greens are either warm or cool. Yellow or sienna may be mixed with the green to make a field warm. Shadows in the trees and ground will be cooler, which suggests the use of a red or a blue mixed with the green to make these areas darker in value.

Warm colors tend to come forward, cool ones to recede. So, in general, the middle distance will be cooler than the foreground, but not as cool as the distance near the horizon. Remember, too, that accents both in value and brilliance of color will tend to be strongest in the foreground. Like most rules, the foregoing has its exceptions. For example, in painting a late afternoon sky against a dark

52

horizon, the horizon area can be the darkest part of the picture and the sky, just above it, the lightest.

SNOW LANDSCAPES

Blue and lavender shadows can turn chaste snows by the brook or under the maple tree into corn faster than anything else. I have often been shocked to observe that such bright shadows do exist on the late afternoon of a winter day; they are almost as bright as some popular snow painters paint them. Nevertheless, blue and lavender is corn, it is chocolate-boxy, and it is wrong. God can do things that we, his puny creatures, should not dare, or care, to try and imitate. Blue shadows on snow and bright sunsets are two of these things—they are better left to the Almighty.

I have painted quite a few snow pictures, and my tones in the snow are grayed with black tints, or with red, yellow, or sepia. These colors give a realistic effect. Observe that forms of snow on fields and hills are usually very simple. A most sparing brush stroke will create all the form necessary.

"Pennsylvania Winter."

special techniques

MANY INTERESTING EFFECTS CAN BE OBTAINED IN A WATER-COLOR PAINTING BY USing the following special, and rather unorthodox, techniques.

Experiment 1. Absorbent Tissues. Figs. 9a and 9b

A quick wash was laid over the whole sky area shown in Fig. 9a, lighter at the horizon and gradually darker at the top. The white clouds and the lighter areas were lifted with absorbent tissues, crumpled into a loose ball, as shown in Fig. 9b. The amount of color lifted depended on the pressure in each instance. Several tissues were used, for once a tissue is soiled with color it will smudge a pure white area if used a second time. (Although not shown in this experiment, a tissue containing the damp lifted color *can* be dabbed on light areas to create new cloud forms of different textures and shapes.) At the extreme top the clouds were too white, so after the original wash was dry I glazed a light tone over this whole region.

The size and shape of the lifted areas can be controlled to a considerable degree by the size and shape of the crumpled tissue. Stay with the sky until the washes are dried beyond the stage of running. During this period, quickly catch runs by continuing to lift and create the cloud shapes you want.

This technique has almost endless possibilities. Remember that a damp tissue will lift color out of a wash better than a dry one. If the wash is very wet, a tissue will pick up all the color, leaving the paper white. As the paper dries, a tissue will pick up less and less color, so you must time your "picking up" to lift just the right amount. The edges created also vary from sharp irregular outlines, when the lifting is done out of very wet washes, to very fuzzy edges when the color has nearly dried into the paper. Highly intrigued with this activity, most students go hog

Fig. 9a. A quick wash was laid over the whole sky area, lighter at the horizon line and gradually darker at the top. The white clouds and lighter areas were lifted with absorbent tissues as shown in Fig. 9b.

Fig. 9b. Obtaining a soft cloud effect by lifting color from the wet wash with absorbent tissues.

Fig. 10. *Effects obtained by using an ink eraser and a razor blade on a wet wash.*

Fig. 11. *Making highlights with a razor blade.*

wild. Enjoy yourself, but don't allow yourself to keep making baggy, fluffy clouds all the time. Keep this technique within bounds.

Experiment 2. Eraser, Razor Blade, and Wet Wash. Figs. 10 and 11

The effects obtained by using an ink eraser on a wet wash are startling. In Fig. 10 a loose, runny wash was laid. The eraser was then applied vigorously where the whites show up and less strongly where the mottled effects appear. The side of the eraser was pushed gently near the horizon line to make the little dark clouds. In this case the paper was bruised sufficiently to cause the wet wash to run into the bruised area. Some of the original washes remain and contrast well to the jagged effects of the erased areas. The razor blade was used to clean up white edges in the sky and to highlight the tree trunks, flowers and grasses in the foreground (see Fig. 11). Forceful, dramatic effects are possible with this eraser technique. However, strong, handmade 140-pound paper or heavier should be used; otherwise holes may be dug through the paper. If changes are necessary, washes can be laid over the light areas or a sponge can be used to scrub out sections to a lighter gray or dirty white. This is a very flexible way of working. When the paper is dry, hard rubbing with an ink eraser will lighten a dark section gradually. Less vigorous rubbing will lighten delicate tones quickly. The razor blade will scratch a finer and cleaner line on dry paper, but strong pressure is needed. If, after the paper is dry, certain spots need to be dug out—for instance, if a new white cloud is desired—a watercolor brush full of water can be laid in those spots and they will lift out easily with an eraser or razor blade, giving a clean edge where the wet wash met the dry paper.

The student should get excitement out of this way of working, and he should practice so that he understands the possibilities. A whole picture can be made in this manner. But, more important, the eraser and razor blade, used discreetly, can enliven surfaces with rich, sudden textures. When I make water colors these tools are always at hand for possible use.

Experiment 3. Foliage: Washes and Dry Brush. Fig. 12

This set of experiments should help break down any barriers of fear the student might have when starting to paint trees and foliage. The variety of textures shown in Fig. 12 was achieved by using brushes in several ways. The light fuzzy grays were made by rubbing and stomping a brush with a little color in it over the white surface. I call this the dry brush method. Different values and amounts of color over various grained papers give a wide assortment of textures. An old stiff bristle brush, with the hairs standing in all directions, was dipped into a full liquid color

Fig. 12. Brush strokes made with a dry brush over dry white paper and with dry and wet brushes on both wet washes and dried areas. The small highlights in the lower right area were picked out with a razor blade; the larger areas of trees were rubbed white with an eraser.

and then touched lightly to the paper to give the sharp spotted blacks. Next the brush with dark color was scumbled into the washed areas. This is one of my favorite ways of working. The hard, sharp areas and the fuzzy forms against the crisp white or in contrast to the softer tones of the washes offer a richness in contrasts which is exciting.

Always consider the beauty of the pure white paper in water coloring. The whites will sing for you when you need the brightest highlights.

Experiment 4. Pen and Ink and Flooded Paper. Fig. 13

In Fig. 13 the paper was stretched, mounted, and left until it was bone dry. Then I flooded the areas where the figures were to be drawn, using a large water-color brush, so that the water stood on the surface of the dry paper. Quickly I drew into this with the pen and black ink. Where the pen dug into the paper a rich, fuzzy black line remained; where the pen touched the paper lightly the ink merged with the water on the paper and fuzzy washes spread. The water has the effect of separating the ink into small spots, and the granular texture you get is stunning. Unfortunately the subtleties are always lost in any photographic reproduction, so try it out for yourself. As the paper dried, the new lines I made became cleaner and less fuzzy; and when the paper was completely dry I added bold sharp lines to give final contrast and variety to the drawing.

You will find this tricky technique interesting, and while experimenting with it you will stumble upon other effects which can be readily utilized in creating the fluffier aspects of bird, beast, and Mother Nature, such as feathers, fur, and foliage.

Consider using light color washes during your experiments with pen and black ink. They are most effective, particularly the yellows and reds. And of course you can draw with colored inks instead of black, or with water colors used like ink, on

Fig. 13. Pen and ink outlines drawn over a wet wash.

Fig. 14. Outlines made with an etching needle.

a pen. Mix a little pool of water color, any color, about the consistency of ink, and it will flow from a pen just as easily. The intensity of the colored inks is greater, however, and may be needed for the stronger accents.

Experiment 5. Etching Needle Technique. Fig. 14

This is great fun to do, and I have made several pictures using this technique alone.

After laying a very wet wash of medium gray, I drew all the lines into the wet paper with an etching needle. (Actually, any sharp-pointed instrument can be used, even the sharp wooden handle of a water-color brush.) The wet color flowed into the lines. After that I took various colors of different intensities and let them flow freely over different sections of the paper. They merged with the gray and with each other. The white spots were dug out with the razor blade when the paper was still wet. If you should want dark lines against white, the original gray wash can be lifted with tissue after the lines are drawn. Also, colors applied over lifted

Fig. 15. Spatter effects.

white areas would be more intense than if they were washed over grayed areas.

Once you get started with this technique you will find it hard to stop. You will keep making discoveries of your own which will go beyond anything shown in Fig. 14. This technique is good for the free and easy approach; it is not good for precisely detailed works.

Experiment 6. Spattering. Fig. 15

The effect of spattering can be so fascinating (and the technique is so quick) that you will probably want to spatter everything from your work sheet to the kitchen floor. After having the usual preliminary fling, start spattering with discretion.

Fig. 15 shows what can be done with a spattered background. The tools used were an old palette knife (a matchstick would also do) and an old toothbrush. Mix some lampblack or black ink in a saucer, dip the toothbrush into the liquid, and hold the brush over the area of paper to be spattered. Then pull the palette knife or matchstick over the bristles of the brush, allowing the resulting spray to fall on the paper. The size of the spots will vary depending on the consistency of the liquid and on the amount of liquid that the brush contains. Thick color mixed with little water will make a fine spray. A full brush loaded with thin color will occasionally leak big drops. Experience will soon teach you how to regulate the amount of liquid for the effect you want, and also how to hold the brush. Areas of the paper not to be spattered can be covered with paper or cardboard cutouts. Rubber cement can also be brushed over areas that are to be free from spattering, and rubbed off after the spattered areas are dry.

The simple abstract shapes in this exercise were made by placing pieces of cardboard and coins on the paper. After some spattering a few of the pieces were shifted to vary the design. Three or four of the black areas were painted in with a brush and then opaque white was spattered over the black.

Another way of getting a coarser spatter effect is to use a piece of screening, such as that used in screen doors, about 4 by 4 inches. Using a large flat brush, cover the screen with a thin wash, then hold it over the paper and blow hard. Also, a 1-inch brush loaded with watery color can be made to drip different sized drops by shaking it gently, or tapping it over a finger.

After you have done some spattering with black and opaque white, the real fun starts with color. Using cheap drawing paper for your experiments, spatter reds over yellow, dark blues over light greens, sepia over grays. Next try four or five colors over each other, first using light colors, then dark colors. After that use washes of different intensities and colors, let them dry, and then spatter. Lastly, flood wet washes onto the paper and immediately spatter a heavy spray into the still wet area and observe the interesting effects which appear.

In picture making there are two basic spatter techniques: An artist can spray onto the clean paper, draw lines and washes over the spatter to create the composition, and later wash out or paint over with heavy color those spatter areas not desired. Secondly—and this is the usual procedure—an artist may build up his composition with lines and masses, then discreetly spatter the areas which may call for this treatment. Lautrec lithographs are a fine example of spattering; so are many of the paintings by Eugene Berman.

Fig. 16. Texture chart.

Texture chart. Fig. 16

The textures shown in Fig. 16 summarize the foregoing experiments. Starting from the top center and going clockwise, the eight triangles show: spattering technique; wet washes over dry pen and ink; pen and ink on very wet wash; eraser and razor blade erasures; dry brush on white paper and dried washes; clouds lifted with absorbent tissues out of a wet wash; etching needle technique; wet brush washes over dry paper.

The variety and sparkle of the original sheet cannot, unfortunately, show up in any type of reproduction, so it must be left to your imagination until you start making your own experiments. Save your sheets for later reference, noting down how you arrived at the effects you like best.

Texture is most important in a painting; and the awareness of what can be done with brush, pen, and the other tools described, will help solve the problem of a dull-looking surface. However, the delight in unique effects solely for their own sake is dangerous. The student bent on spectacular effects can easily lose sight of the other important qualities—design, drawing, and color. A picture is about something you feel to be important, and texture should contribute to the whole, never become an end in itself.

Once you have learned all you can from these experiments, hold a tight rein on the dizzy charms of textures; save them for the right time and place. Even practicing artists, who should know better, are often tempted too far, and it becomes clear that texture and a nice sense of pattern and color are their chief, if not their whole, motivation for a painting. This tickling of the sensations has become a passing fashion in art; but, as we all know perfectly well, unless a painting also stirs the emotions it will never rank as a true work of art.

"Lake in the Garden of the Gods." Water color.

"Mountain at St. Elmo." Water color.

"Market Place, Port de la Cruz." Water color.

"Central Park Winter." Water color.

a water color, step by step

The seven illustrations, figs. 17 to 23, show actual steps in the development of a water-color landscape. This is one of many possible approaches. Sometimes I leave the sky until the painting is nearly finished, and often I start with the darkest colors rather than the lighter tones. So don't think you have to copy this or any other method exactly. The step-by-step photographs do, however, demonstrate my usual procedure, which I think is as good as any other, and they may help to clarify the text.

"PENNSYLVANIA HILLS"

It would be hard for me to name a favorite area for landscape painting. Wherever I am seems to be my favorite at that particular moment. However, central Pennsylvania is a region I always find myself eager to visit again.

The painting "Pennsylvania Hills" (shown in color in Fig. 23, page 73) was put together from two sketches which I made in the same neighborhood. In leafing through my sketch book I took a great delight in the foreground detail of the typical Pennsylvania farmyard as seen in Fig. 17. But I also had an impulse to show the fat, pale-green, rolling hills with their speckles of trees, and to depict a barn rising upward against higher blue-green hills, ending in the sky. The second sketch (Fig. 18) gave me the lines and color notes I needed. Little effort was needed to combine the two sketches into one composition. The result is shown in the quick, lightly done drawing on water-color paper in Fig. 19. After the drawing was finished, the paper was soaked for fifteen minutes in the bathtub and stretched on a board, all excess water having been removed with a tissue. I allowed the paper to dry for several hours, for I wanted the water color to have the clean fresh effects that are best attained on a dry paper.

Fig. 17. Sketch from the author's notebook. The sketch and color notes were made outdoors; later the details were used in the water color, "Pennsylvania Hills."

Fig. 18. A second sketch, details of which were also used in the "Pennsylvania Hills" composition.

Fig. 19. *Preliminary sketch on water-color paper combining elements from the sketches shown in Figs. 17 and 18.*

Fig. 20. During this stage the sky was established and I brushed a quick wash of very thin May green into the foreground. In the middle distance a touch of chromium oxide dull green was added. A considerable amount of the light pale green remained in the finished picture, helping to pull all the greens together.

The sky was painted with a 1-inch brush charged with a full load of a light tint of black mixed with a vague touch of cadmium red. Starting at the hilltops, I laid the wash upward, darkening the values a bit, eliminating the red tint, and mixing black with a touch of Payne's gray and Winsor blue. This wash was carried to the top margin.

The white clouds were then lifted out of the wet washes with dampened pieces of tissue. During this period I watched the sky carefully to see how the clouds formed. The washes often flow differently from the way you expect, making it necessary to lift out more of the wash. Whatever happens, it is most important to make the cloud formations relate to the whole compositional plan.

Fig. 21. Eager to fix the relationship of sky to earth, I next laid in the distant hills. First I put down a medium heavy wash of Hooker's green mixed with May

69

Fig. 20. The first light wash. Note the cloud effects, achieved by mopping the sky with tissues, and the white area left through the center within the outlines of the buildings and in the lake at left.

green and a touch of Winsor blue. Dark blue-greens were added to these washes as they were drying; toward the end of the drying period some of the dark accents of pure Hooker's green were laid in without mixing with water. With water, Hooker's green, standing alone, becomes a poisonous green color which looks unnatural in a landscape.

The dark field in the middle left area was laid in with a black and Aurora yellow mixture which, when it dried, developed into a grayed, light olive green. Quite a strong Aurora yellow wash covered the right lower foreground. With the corner of a razor blade, I dug out white spots for textural highlights.

Fig. 22. The area of water at the lower left of the picture was given a tint similar to that of the sky. After this, the forms of the hills were developed, mostly with a darker shade of chromium oxide dull green and a touch of black. More trees were added to the middle distance. I was then ready to relate the buildings

70

Fig. 21. Establishing the horizon line and relating colors in foreground.

to the land. The reds of the brick house and the old barns were the main colors used. The big barn was painted a pinkish red; the smaller buildings were painted with blacks and sepia reds as well. The foreground foliage was scumbled in with a dry brush dipped in May green and chromium oxide dull green.

Fig. 23 shows the finished water-color painting, "Pennsylvania Hills." The bright yellow field of the foreground looked quite terrible at the end of the preceding stage. It did not relate to the other colors and it fought with the greens. So I scrubbed it hard with a sponge and, finally, with a cloth, until this whole area was back to a smudgy, dirty, textured white. Then, while it was still very damp, I laid in the pale May green. It was too bright, so I killed the brilliance with an olive-green mixture of chromium oxide dull green and sepia. Later, as the washes dried, grasses were painted in and flower forms were dug out with a razor blade. The chickens were touched in with opaque white.

71

Fig. 22. Filling in with reds and pinks for the buildings, and scrubbing and washing in the green tree outlines.

The reflections in the water at the left were developed, echoing the red of the barn and the greens of the trees. The roofs were bluish and gray. The foliage was built up, adding new darks of pure, thick Hooker's green out of the tube for the two big evergreens.

All things considered, I had quite good luck with this water color, for it was made under tension, with the photographer waiting to photograph each step before I could proceed with the next. The only real trouble I had was with the foreground, which turned out with a different texture and color than would have been attained if everything had gone smoothly. However, I think that this was yet another instance when an accident turned into an asset.

Materials Used in Executing "Pennsylvania Hills"

Paper:

Whatman 140-pound cold press, cut to size; 20 by 28 inches

Colors of palette:

Chromium oxide dull green (Grumbacher)

Fig. 23. The finished painting, "Pennsylvania Hills."

Permanent green pale [May green] (Grumbacher)
Hooker's green dark (Winsor & Newton)
Winsor blue (Winsor & Newton)
Aurora yellow (Winsor & Newton)
Cadmium red (Winsor & Newton)
Alizarin crimson (Winsor & Newton)
Sepia (Winsor & Newton)
Payne's gray (Grumbacher)
Black (Grumbacher)
White (Shiva Casein)

Brushes:

One 1-inch flat water-color brush
One ½-inch flat water-color brush
One ¼-inch flat water-color brush
Three round brushes: 1 medium, 1 small, 1 very small

"Caribbean Sunset." Water color.

"The Great God Pan." Water color.

"Birds of Paradise." Ink and water color.

"Threshing in Minnesota." Water color.

gouache painting

GOUACHE IS JUST AS MUCH A WATER COLOR AS THE KIND OF TRANSPARENT PAINTING commonly referred to under that name. Though the word has a different connotation, gouache is still pigment and water applied to paper. To avoid confusion, transparent water color is sometimes called aquarelle; and as long as we are prepared to tangle with one French word, gouache, we may as well go along with the second one, too. For the purposes of this chapter at least, let's designate the transparent water-color method described in the earlier part of the book as aquarelle, and the method described here, gouache. An example of the latter is shown in Fig. 24.

There are degrees of transparency and opacity in a water color and it is often hard to tell at just what point an aquarelle becomes a gouache. The minute one starts mixing white with the transparent pigments one goes in the opaque direction of gouache. Some transparent tube pigments are quite opaque when used in full force with little water. When even the more transparent pigments are used very thick, or when several washes are laid one over another, the colors lose their transparency and really come close to the opacity of gouache. On water color juries I have seen several professional artists have great difficulty in agreeing on the classification of a certain work as an aquarelle or a gouache. But this, I think, is the least of our worries.

There are special colors on the market which are used for gouache painting. The manufacturers may call these by different names, such as tempera, casein, gouache, or opaque water color, as well as poster and showcard color. These colors are basically the same as those used in aquarelle, with an added filler which gives the color more body and opacity. They are mixed with water and are quick-drying. The opacity of the color negates the power of the paper itself to affect

77

the color. For that reason, the student who has been painting in water color will find that there must be a switch in his thinking when he applies gouache colors. Actually, after he experiments with the opaque color, he will probably find it easier to work with than aquarelle. The beauty of aquarelle is its transparency and the deft calligraphic touch. When worked over, aquarelle tends to lose its freshness. In gouache, working over and changing adds new effects, often unexpected, often richer in texture, body, and color.

In passing, let it be said that these gouache colors mixed with much water can also become transparent, so that a transparent water color, an aquarelle, can in fact be painted with them. I have done this quite successfully. Probably, however, we would find somewhat less transparency and crispness if we were actually to compare such a result with a similar study done in the best aquarelle colors.

Bruce Mitchell, generally thought of as a gouache painter, uses transparent water colors to get transparent skies or watery effects which contrast nicely with the heavy opaques of other elements painted in gouache.

If you have read the first section of the book on transparent water-color painting, you can see that there is an easy and natural transition from aquarelle to gouache painting, and the odds are that you are going to have a fine time doing it. You may also wish to linger en route, combining transparent color effects with opaque, gradually going more in the latter direction.

For the beginner in gouache who has already practiced with aquarelle, I suggest the following experiments to get acquainted with the new medium quickly. (Some people may wish to start with gouache, and it is not a bad idea, for it is easier than aquarelle. Even so, I hope these readers will also study the section on water colors, do enough of those exercises to learn how to lay a wash, and read those sections on combining colors.)

Experiment 1.

Lay thin washes on paper or illustration board.

Experiment 2.

Lay medium heavy washes and pure color out of the tube over the original thin washes while they are still wet. Observe how the thin and thick washes merge. Do this with the same color and then with the other colors of your palette.

Experiment 3.

Lay light and heavy washes over the thin dry washes; see how utterly different the effect is. Timing is almost as important in gouache as it is in aquarelle painting.

Fig. 24. Gouache painting. Note the opacity of the painted areas in comparison to those in the water color in Fig. 23. Below: Fig. 24a. "Caribbean Merchants." Gouache.

Experiment 4.

Lay a thick heavy wash of color and, while wet, quickly lay into it washes thinned with much water. Do this with the same color. Do it with other colors.

Experiment 5.

Lay another heavy wash and let it dry. Then work over it with thin washes of the same color and with other colors. Observe how different this result is from that in experiment 4.

Experiment 6.

Repeat experiments 4 and 5 with full, heavy colors over the two washes, wet and dry.

Experiment 7.

Lay one heavy wash over another after each has dried; see if it takes evenly. Some brands of gouache color pick up; that is, the first coat does not adhere to the paper well enough and the original color lifts. This makes for a messy effect when applying two or more layers and can cause a great deal of difficulty; there seems little to do about it except try to curb your impatience. I have had fine results with Shiva casein colors * in this respect, and have put many layers over each other—in fact, in one instance, I laid nine skies before achieving the right one.

The sensuous love of color should give the student so much excitement that he will eagerly try playing with the whole range of colors. Observe especially what happens to color when you mix white with it; see what a touch of black does to green and yellow and how a little black and white will change the character of any color. This quick random play with color can go on endlessly. As the student develops he may find, at times, that he is in a rut; and by going back to this play with color, he can revitalize his color imagination and gaily start down new paths of color harmonies.

Gouache pigment has a soft, ingratiating quality. Its pastel effect seems to make easy the achievement of good color relationships. However, it can also be dull. Sharp contrasts of color and value can keep this dullness in check. Calligraphic drawing into the flat colors can be most effective, and all the technical tricks of creating texture outlined earlier in this book can be used. Try exercises in

* *See notes on materials, pages 82-86.*

scumbling with the dry brush. Try the ink eraser; experiment with the razor blade, using both its flat surface and its sharp corner over wet and dry surfaces. Absorbent tissues will give most unusual effects by lifting the wet color. And try bristle brushes or a sponge for wiping out areas of color, either going back to the original white of the paper or taking off just enough of the top surface to leave a smudged color underneath.

Drawing the structural lines of the composition with genuine black waterproof ink, thus creating thin and heavy lines and black areas on the white paper, is one way to work, and it is interesting and easy for the beginner. After the ink is dry, apply the colors freely, covering the black ink where desired with thick or thin pigment and leaving the black in other places. The glazing of thin color over the black gives a different texture and color. Later any part of the picture can be washed out; the ink lines will remain and the artist can start over with his painting. Ink can be laid over the color, but if the opaque color is very thick and smooth the ink often flakes off. This is particularly true of very thick ink.

The student who starts with the gouache section must realize that nearly everything written in the section on transparent water colors pertains to gouache as well.

materials and equipment for gouache

To BE CONSISTENT WITH THE FIRST PART OF THE BOOK, WE SHOULD HAVE DISCUSSED materials for gouache painting before technique. It seemed logical, however, to reverse the procedure here, and also in the next section on casein, for most readers will be more ready to check their equipment once they have understood the technical differences and the new effects they are shooting at as they move from one related medium to the next.

PAPER AND ILLUSTRATION BOARDS

Most of the materials used for aquarelle can be used in gouache. Among the papers, heavy water-color paper is best, stretched and taped down on a drawing board. Use 140-pound paper or heavier. The student can experiment with different papers, even with thinner papers; but as a rule he will find the thinner papers, while taking semiopaque colors quite satisfactorily, will wilt under heavier applications of gouache.

More commonly, illustration boards are used for gouache. If an illustration board is thin, it can be tacked to the drawing board or taped with gummed tape or strong masking tape. The masking tape has the advantage that it can be removed after the picture is done, leaving a clean white margin, whereas the dirty gummed tape covered with color is unsightly and cannot be removed easily.

The really heavy illustration boards, such as those made by Whatman or Winsor & Newton, are fine; and they are stiff enough without being fastened to a board. If a board bends from much wet color, wet the back and put the board under an evenly distributed weight, such as a pile of books, until it dries flat. Another advantage of the heavy illustration board is that the paper used is usually handmade; it is much tougher than the cheap illustration board and can be scrubbed and scratched without ill effects. These boards usually come in two sizes, 22 by 30 inches and 26 by 39 inches. Their only drawback, I would say, is their high cost. However, if you don't like your first painting, the same board can be used again by covering it up with one or more coats of casein. The boards come in smooth or rough texture. The rougher board is more effective for dry brush techniques and creating textures; the smooth board allows for slickness, neatness, and more detail. Masonite boards and gesso panels are also used occasionally for gouache, and are described in some detail in the section on casein, for which medium they are particularly recommended.

BRUSHES

All your water-color brushes can be used for gouache. In addition, I often use ¼-inch and ½-inch soft-haired oil painting brushes and, occasionally, stiff bristle brushes, which are good for scrubbing out small areas. Old bristle brushes with bristles sticking out in all directions come in handy for textural effects. A large, flat 2-inch house-painter's brush is fine for covering large areas.

It is even more important to clean out your brushes thoroughly after using casein paint, for the binder in the color has greater adhesive strength than in aquarelle. Warm water and soap will do the job well. The warmer the water, the easier the cleaning will be, but continuous use of very hot water will eventually ruin the brushes—so watch out. You might keep a glass jar containing a liquid detergent, such as Glim or Joy, near your washstand. Dip the brush in the detergent, then rinse out with warm water. If paint has dried hard in the brush, let it soak in warm, soapy water. Denatured alcohol also cuts dried casein well.

PIGMENTS

Among the best-known trade names for colors used in gouache painting are: Winsor & Newton, Grumbacher, Schminke, Boucour, Weber, and Shiva.

I have not worked with all of these colors. I was led to the Shiva casein paints originally and found them so good that I have used them almost exclusively. This brand is popular with many artists, but there are those who think just as highly of the other brands. I recommend that you try out the various makes of colors and decide for yourself. One or more of these reputable brands can be found in any local artists' materials store, except, possibly, the Shiva colors. These, however, can be ordered directly from the company: Ramon Shiva, 433 Goethe Street, Chicago, Illinois. If you write them, ask for a price list and literature on the use of their medium.

Some gouache paints dry very quickly, like the Shiva colors; others, like Grumbacher, are made to dry more slowly, and some artists find this an advantage. The expensive colors are a good investment, as they are more permanent; the pigment is usually more powerful and lays better. Showcard colors fade more quickly; they may be used for your first experimental steps in gouache if you wish to save money, but later, for serious picture making, you should certainly get the more permanent paints.

My own palette varies greatly, depending on the subject and how I wish to treat it. Here is one I frequently use for landscape work:

Lampblack or ivory black	*Yellow ocher*
Titanium white	*Cadmium red light*
Cobalt or cerulean blue	*Alizarin crimson*
Ponsol blue	*Venetian red*
Chromium oxide dull green	*Burnt sienna*
Cadmium green	*Burnt or raw umber*
Cadmium yellow medium	

Often I use fewer colors, and it is recommended that the beginner do the same. A good starter palette would be:

Black	*Cadmium yellow*
White	*Cadmium red*
Cobalt blue	*Burnt umber*
Chromium oxide dull green	

Later try different colors in place of these, and gradually add more as you find you need them.

There are certain colors I like to use for special purposes. Orange, which can be raw, can also sing tremendously; mixed with white this color gives what I call a hot pink. Shiva green is very powerful and poisonous; mixed with white, it makes a cold, almost bluish, artificial color, quite exciting for certain effects. Naples yellow is a modest, cool, and weak color; mixed with other colors it tempers them in a quiet way. Payne's gray is very intense, harsh, cold, and bluish. Indian red is a coolish and heavy earth color. Terra verte is a quiet, weak sister of chromium oxide dull green, and has its use in landscapes where many different greens are required.

The student should observe the great difference between the three cadmium yellows, how pale and cool the light cadmium, how stridently hot the deep yellow.

84

The same is true of the three cadmium reds. Notice the power of the alizarin red—when painted thickly, it gets blackish; yet when used thinly and with a touch of white, a screaming, cold pink appears. Observe the different pinks obtained by using cadmium red light.

CARE OF YOUR COLORS

Gouache colors dry rapidly, so squeeze out small portions as you need them and replace the caps on the tubes. A drop or two of water touched over the colors with the brush will help keep them soft for a couple of hours or so on the palette. Always keep the tubes tightly covered, for the pigment cannot be restored once a tube dries out. Don't keep the colors in freezing temperatures.

PALETTE AND WATER JAR

My palette is the same as I use for water-color painting—a large white plate. Actually I use two, as noted earlier. A large white porcelain tray would be good, too; or you could use a cooky tin or a piece of thick glass placed on a white board. When cleaning dry paint off the palette, cut off all lumps of pigment with a razor blade, then wash off the remainder with a rag or tissues. Never let your palette get too full of dirty color while working.

A large one- or two-quart jar with a wide opening is best for water. And change it often.

WORK TABLE

The same requirements apply here as for aquarelle painting. In the beginning, if washes run, I work with the board flat on the table. Later I prop it up at a 25- or 35-degree angle, so I can see better what I am doing (see Fig. 1). Good light is important; and the light should come from the left if you are right-handed and from the right if you are left-handed. For night work I have an eight-foot fluorescent light, nine feet from the floor above my table. This enables me to see the palette and my picture under exactly the same light and with no shadows cast by my hand. These conditions approximate daylight and make night painting—whether in gouache or aquarelle—a pleasure, with little strain on the eyes.

MATS FOR WORKING

It is a good idea to have several mats with openings cut to the size paper you usually work with. When the picture nears completion you can lay the mat over it, thus enclosing the painting, cutting off rough edges, and setting off your work to its best advantage. Every artist needs cheering up, and a mat gives the work a new look, a final professional touch that is most heartening.

FRAMING AND MATTING WATER COLORS AND GOUACHE PAINTINGS

Water colors and gouache paintings are framed by the same method. To protect the surface from dust and dirt, the picture must be covered with glass. If the artist cannot have a good framer do his framing (and, sad to state, there are many bad framers), he can make his own frames. The usual way to do this is to cut a mat out of strong mat board or Celotex, cutting the opening with a beveled edge. A special knife can be bought for this purpose in the art supply store, or a razor blade may be used. You will also need a set square to cut straight lines at right angles. A large margin of four or five inches presents most pictures handsomely, although if the frame is to be rather wide, a narrower mat works well. The mat can be white or painted a discreet neutral tint with flat gouache. Linen mats are also very handsome.

The frame may measure from one to four inches wide, depending on the size and nature of the picture. Sometimes the natural wood will be just right; or it can be stained and waxed, or painted and waxed.

Remember the purpose of the frame is to set off the picture; the frame should enclose it discreetly. Often a beautiful and ornate frame distracts from the picture. In museums one sees old masters in frames that fight with the paintings.

Also, in an effort to have the frame harmonize with the colors in the picture, framers tend to carry the same colors into the frame too much; this makes for monotony. A neutralized, grayed tone, perhaps of an opposing color to the dominant one in the picture, might be more successful.

I suggest you study the different methods of framing seen in exhibitions, where you will get many ideas. Water colors sent to exhibitions *must* be framed and under glass.

"Winter Day in Key West." Gouache.

"The Great Middle West." Gouache.

"Processional." Gouache.

"Old Farm near Lewisburg." Casein.

casein painting

A SIMILAR PROBLEM ARISES IN DIFFERENTIATING BETWEEN CASEIN PAINTING AND gouache as arose when we compared gouache with aquarelle. Casein painting is really one aspect of gouache; one might say it is gouache carried a step farther, to the point where the effect approaches that of an oil painting. After the painting has been developed with thin washes, or with washes of the consistency of cream, paint can be applied more heavily; any number of coats can be laid on, one over the other. Little or no water need be used with the application of the pigment. This applies particularly to the Shiva colors. The palette knife, brush, or even a matchstick can be used to create scumbled rough lines and textured areas with globs of thick color as it comes from the tube. The resulting surface has the rich body and weight of an oil painting and lends itself to varnishing and waxing after the pigment has dried. Such pictures can be framed in the same way as oil paintings. All this makes it difficult, sometimes impossible, for even professional painters to tell the difference between the two mediums.

The odds are also good that the casein painting will remain as it is painted longer than the average study in oil. Masonite board is longer lasting than canvas; and there will be no cracking of pigment, a common defect in oil painting when there is the lack of a good medium. Furthermore, casein colors will remain fresh and bright and will not gray down so easily. Whether all this will please or displease our grandchildren is a question which we will leave to them.

Casein dries quickly. A few minutes after application a new coat can be laid over the previous one. One need never be slowed down like the oil painter who must put his painting away to dry for a day or more whenever his paint gets too thick or sticky.

Actually, the casein paint does not become bone dry for a long time. After

89

a week one can still take off a little color by rubbing hard with a wet cloth. But after six months, and certainly after a year, the paint is impervious to wetness.

PAINTING THE PICTURE

One can begin a gouache or casein with the board flat on the table, as in water color. In fact, when using big, wet washes to get the board covered quickly, this is the easiest way, for the washes will not run too much. Assuming you next wish to develop the painting, using paint of a thick consistency, you can set the board up on a table or an easel and work just as in oil painting. Actually, for small paintings, it is not necessary to have an easel; an old straight-backed chair will do. But pictures 24 by 36 inches or larger should be painted on an easel for convenience and comfort in working.

If you have gone through the experimental exercises of the gouache and water color sections it will not be necessary to do many more experiments before you are well acquainted with the casein medium.

I suggest that you take the pigment as it comes from the tube and experiment with the palette knife. Make flat surfaces and try to draw with it. Interesting, coarse, irregular effects are attained this way. Work it thin and thick. Take globs of the pigment and let them stand on the surface so that they give a bas relief effect. These should not stand more than ⅛ inch above the surface; if they are thicker they may break off when dry.

Next, mix the pigment with a little water and observe how you can smear it around with the palette knife or finger. Dip small brushes and old, worn ones into the pigment and experiment with them. The resulting lines cannot be controlled easily, but you will find the technique valuable for spontaneous and lively effects. With a very fine, pointed brush, a controlled line is possible if the pigment is well mixed with water.

One of the difficulties of the casein medium as opposed to oil painting is that one cannot blend the colors at leisure. Blending must be done rapidly while the quick-drying colors are still wet. This limitation at least keeps one from being too slick.

Take the pointed handle of the brush and draw into the wet pigment with the wood; exciting linear effects can be created this way. Interesting textural effects can be obtained by scraping the color off a damp area with the palette knife. Glazing thin washes over heavy, dried-in color will also provide a most surprising range of subdued effects with variations of color that one would not imagine possible. A wet rag can be dragged over the already dried-in, but not bone dry, color, and it will smudge. With more pressure, the various colors will blur into each other until a general allover tone covers the whole board; then new delineations of color can be applied over this.

If your painting proves unsatisfactory, a thick coat of white or any other color can be laid quickly over the entire painting, giving you a new surface to work on. If the earlier painting had a heavy impasto, you may be provided with an interesting, rough texture on which to work. If it is too rough, sand down the surface and watch, as you do so, for interesting abstract arrangements of colors in the underpainting that can be utilized in a new design. In other words, don't sand down any farther than necessary.

Freshly painted casein color will dry in to a different color, and the extent of this change can be quite astonishing. For instance, a not-too-thick wash laid over a darker color may at first look very light and bright, but as the wash dries it usually takes on the character of the darker color. The wash is absorbed by the dark color. After years of experience I find I am still surprised by these changes. They can be most inconvenient at times, particularly if one wishes to match a color. As an experiment, mix a puddle of color and lay it thickly on a board. As the color dries, paint into the dried pigment with the same color and brush and see how it is *not* the same! The only way to have the area even is to repaint it all, not just a section of it. To compensate for this trickiness, the uncertainty of the exact hue of the pigment when it has dried frequently brings attractive chance effects.

When starting a painting, you may find it helpful to get away from the white surface of your board at once. Cover the whole area with quite a thick coat of any color which appeals to you and suits the theme of your painting. Black, and even a dead gray, can be effective, but also be sure to try bright cadmium red, a hot yellow, and a somber umber. Draw your compositional structure into this background color, using a small brush and any color you desire. Don't be too careful. Feel your way. Consider all your lines as tentative for, unlike those in aquarelle, they can be changed later if necessary. The nature of casein is such that building one color over another enriches it. As you develop the painting your background will gradually be covered, will in itself be destroyed; yet, from underneath, it will continue to pull your whole color scheme into a happy relationship. Sometimes you may leave certain areas of the background color uncovered, or you may reinstate it in certain passages as the picture develops.

Remember that thin washes glazed over a powerful color will temper it slightly, often giving delightful and unexpected effects. Casein painting is an exciting, sensuous affair, but don't allow yourself to be led astray too far by the color. Be sure that form and texture play their proper roles, too.

Results in casein can be quick and effective, yet I find that I generally spend from three to five times as long on a casein painting as I do on an aquarelle. The awareness that laying one color over another will give greater texture, plasticity, and weight encourages a slower development of the picture, whereas in transparent water color one plans a color, puts it down quickly, and can do only a limited amount of revision.

Like painters in oil, casein painters must be prepared to face the fact that the medium offers a great temptation to overwork a picture. You may work very hard, even with passion, for days on end, then cherish a painting as the repository of this agonized (and surely artistic!) effort. Never confuse labor with the esthetic worth of a painting. Not even experienced artists know the value of their work until after a cooling-off period. Set your newest painting aside, hide it for a week, preferably a month, then look at it with a fresh eye. If it still seems good, leave it; if not so good, decide whether or not it has possibilities for repainting. If it has none, first profit by learning from its better features and its mistakes, then permit yourself no misgivings at putting an axe to it. Your next painting should be better.

VARNISHING THE FINISHED PICTURE

When varnishing a casein painting, I find the following procedure gives excellent results:

Isolation of casein with varnish:

Shiva ethereal varnish is first applied over the surface of the painting by means of an atomizer such as is used with fixative on charcoal drawings.

Varnishing:

1. After the ethereal varnish is thoroughly dry, reduce the Shiva glazing varnish with an equal amount (by volume) of rectified turpentine and use this for the first coat of varnish.

2. After an interval of two or three days, use the glazing varnish without thinning for the second coat.

3. Should the painting look spotty after two or three days, apply a third coat of varnish.

It is important that the varnish application be done with a wide, soft brush; the varnish should be put on as quickly as possible and not rubbed or dragged over the surface.

"Up in the Sky." Casein.
(Courtesy Abbott Laboratories)

"Snow Mountain." Casein.

"Springtime in Connecticut." Casein.

"Prudence and Scarlet." Casein.

"Haitian Ballet."

(Notes on making a painting are given at the end of the following chapter on materials.)

CASEIN AND OIL PAINTING

Many painters today like the technique of underpainting with casein mixed with water, then glazing with oil paint. The student who has painted in oil may find this procedure appealing. It can produce very subtle and rich effects.

Develop the picture just as you would any casein painting to a point you consider favorable, then let it dry for at least two hours. Apply a thin coat of ethereal varnish over the painting. This acts as an isolator between the two types of pigment. Allow to dry.

Mix the oil colors to the desired color hue and reduce the color with glazing varnish to approximate the color value desired as a glaze over the casein painting. Apply thinly. The glazing varnish acts as a medium to vary the color value as well the hue. The oil color thinned with turpentine will make a transparent glaze which will dry quickly. Always allow a period of at least twelve hours for the oil colors and glazing varnish to set if you wish to paint with casein again. This procedure may be repeated until the painting is completed. For correctional purposes, casein which has been applied over glazes may be wiped off immediately with a damp cloth. Likewise, oil glazes which have been applied over casein may be removed with turpentine without affecting the original underpainting.

materials for casein painting

ALL THE INFORMATION ON MATERIALS AND THEIR USES AS GIVEN FOR GOUACHE APPLY to casein painting. And here are a few additional notes:

MASONITE BOARDS AND GESSO PANELS

Masonite board, cut to size, and then covered with two or three coats of commercial casein that comes in quart or gallon cans, is probably the favorite working surface. It is sympathetic to brush and paint, and is durable and cheap. Various companies make casein for use as a primer. I have used Luminal successfully. Paint both sides of the board, so that it will not warp. Generally the smoother side is used for the picture, but the rough one can be used just as well if you like its texture. When a very smooth surface is desired, sandpaper each coat after the priming dries. Fine steel wool will give a sleek, polished surface to the final coat. Personally, I prefer the rough tooth of the painted surface, so I usually do not sandpaper. I like to make up several boards at once; it saves time, and they are ready whenever I need them.

Gesso panels are also good for casein painting. These can be bought in many art supply stores. I suggest you purchase a few small ones; if this surface with its greater absorbency appeals to you, later, to save money, you can do your own gessoing on Masonite board. Here is Albert Christ-Janer's recipe for a gesso, which I have found excellent:

Materials:

Rabbit-skin glue (or any gelatinous glue recommended by your paint dealer)
Gilder's whiting
Zinc white powder
Sun-thickened linseed oil (optional)
A double boiler
One inexpensive varnish brush

Step 1. To make a primer for gesso: Put 1 pint water in the double boiler. Add 2 sheets rabbit-skin glue (or 1 cup broken rabbit-skin glue). Heat to the boiling point, but do not boil. When the glue is melted, apply the liquid glue to both sides of your panel. This layer of glue is essential as a base, or primer, for subsequent layers of gesso.

Step 2. To make gesso: Combine equal parts zinc white powder and liquid glue (made in the above proportion), stirring constantly. Then add 1 part Gilder's whiting; continue to stir. Maintain heat just below boiling. If desired, add 1 tablespoon sun-thickened linseed oil and stir constantly until the oil is absorbed by the solution. The addition of the oil will help prevent possible chipping.

As this solution heats, evaporation takes place. Add water sparingly to maintain a consistency of heavy cream; never let the solution get as thin as milk.

The formula will be sufficient for one panel 18 by 24 inches, allowing one coat for the back and three or four coats for the front. Obviously much time will be saved if a number of Masonite panels are treated at one time, so increase the measures given in proportion to the number of panels you wish to cover.

Heavy water-color boards such as those made by Whatman or Winsor & Newton are also fine for casein paintings up to 22 by 30 inches. Some artists also use canvas and find it satisfactory. I have done this but rarely, for I prefer the hard surface and durability of the boards. Actually, casein will adhere to practically any surface, but the thinner water-color papers are not good for laying on heavy paint; the bending paper will easily crack a thick impasto.

BRUSHES

Be sure your basic equipment includes:

1. One large, flat 1½-inch bristle brush for laying in big areas quickly.
2. At least six bristle brushes, from ¾-inch to the smallest size.
3. Six soft-haired oil painting brushes from ¾-inch to the smallest size.

With these brushes on hand, experience will soon show you which size and kind you need for the various maneuvers.

PALETTE KNIFE

This is a particularly important weapon for the casein technique. A good-sized one with a rounded tip and a smaller one with a fine pointed tip will be sufficient for most purposes.

VARNISH

Shiva ethereal varnish and Shiva glazing varnish, used as outlined on page 92 give highly satisfactory results.

Shiva has a casein emulsion which some artists like to use. The student, after he has worked with casein for a time, should try it. In using it with your casein pigments, use one part emulsion to five parts water. If more emulsion is used the colors become milky.

Shiva Media is used as a retouch varnish and thinner for oil colors. Use one part Shiva Media to four parts turpentine. When this is used as a thinner, the painting maintains an equalized finish. Other varnishes may be equally good for different brands of casein paint, and I suggest you check with a reliable artists' material store and try out their suggestions.

WAX

Wax is sometimes used as a final cover, after the varnish, and it gives a rich-looking finish.

Ozenfant's Original Picture Preserver and Grumbacher's White Wax in jars can be bought at artists' materials stores. I have found both satisfactory.

Shiva has recommended Simonize also, for it has a high content of carnauba wax.

If you wish, you can make your own wax preparation by the following formula:

1½ ounces (by weight) white beeswax

4½ ounces rectified turpentine

Mix in a double boiler. After making sure the painting is dry, brush the warm mixture very thinly onto the surface. Let dry two or three days, then polish. To secure a greater sheen, a small amount of Damar varnish may be added.

a casein painting, step by step

EVERYONE MARVELS AT THE BEAUTIFUL BALANCE THAT THE WOMEN OF THE TROPICS maintain with their heavily laden baskets. In Haiti I wondered at this balance, at the gestures of the women, and the great loads they carried on their heads. After making a number of sketches, it delighted me to flatter this astonishing capacity of theirs by adding more baskets, fruits, and birds—more than even these women could possibly carry. My joy in getting away from a literal interpretation led to amusing distortions and a free play of color.

"CARIBBEAN EQUILIBRIUM"

Fig. 25. This pencil sketch was the first step in the development of the painting and was done from imagination. I had drawn hundreds of figures in Haiti, and made several variations on this theme, so I felt no need to refer to the sketches from life.

Fig. 26. Using the sketch in Fig. 25 as a starting point, I again drew the two figures, this time on the casein-primed Masonite board, changing their proportions and making more of the upper part of the composition in which the baskets and birds appear. This drawing was done with the utmost freedom and speed; I was feeling my way and knew that the black-red color I started with would be covered as the colors of the design developed. It so happened in this case that I liked the disposition of lines and masses so well that I stuck fairly close to them until the finish. If this had not been so, I could still have made basic changes at this stage of the painting.

Fig. 27. From the beginning I had in mind a particular color scheme which I wanted to develop, and luckily it turned out the way I envisioned it. I planned a light, whitish-blue background with white-robed figures and umber or red-black faces and arms. Sharp accents of hot yellow, orange, and red were to be used

Fig. 25. Preliminary sketch for the gouache, "Caribbean Equilibrium."

Fig. 26. The start of the gouache painting.

Fig. 27. Color and textures are developed; shapes become a little clearer.

Fig. 28. The finished gouache painting.

with heavy dark green, to create excitement of pattern. With great freedom and almost careless brushing in of color, I covered the original lines and washes shown in Fig. 26 with the above-mentioned color. Opaque titanium white was laid into the white paper areas of the dresses, and grayed tones suggesting folds and forms were drawn into these whites.

Supposing the design were to have been left at this stage, as a finished picture, it could have been framed with glass and classified as a gouache. Unlike a water color with transparent washes, the color was thick enough to be almost entirely opaque, yet it still did not have the body and texture which a continued laying on of pigments achieves in a full-fledged casein painting.

Fig. 28. This fourth step takes the goauche painting and develops it into what we designate as a casein painting. The reader will have realized that this is a somewhat arbitrary distinction, for the picture is still a gouache, only painted more heavily. However, this thickly painted opaque method, which is generally varnished and waxed, is what is known as a casein painting. It looks far closer to an oil painting than to a water color.

Considering the design as it stood in Fig. 27, I felt the color could be refined and enriched. Also, I wanted a finer consideration of detail that would create more convincing forms and subtler space relationships.

The blue background was painted over several times before it arrived at the final stage. Thin washes were glazed over thicker layers of paint, and the palette knife was used to scumble with thick color. The palette knife and a small, thick bristle brush that lifted the pure color without water were used extensively in drawing richer reds and oranges into the fruits and baskets. New whites and thick, pure orange were also drawn into the figures with the same brush and palette knife. A small water-color brush with fluid color was used for details and accents.

The finished picture was varnished like an oil painting to make it more brilliant. After the varnish dried, I applied wax as an additional protection and to soften the hard, shiny varnish. Waxing cuts the glare of reflected light so that a picture can be viewed easily from different positions and under various lighting conditions. The painting, framed and hung like an oil, is indistinguishable from a work done in that medium.

Materials Used in "Caribbean Equilibrium"

Board: Masonite board, 12 by 16 inches, covered with three coats of Luminal casein paint

Colors of palette (all Shiva casein):

Cerulean blue

Cadmium greens

Chrome oxide green No. 2 deep

Cadmium yellow medium

Cadmium orange

Cadmium red extra scarlet

Alizarin crimson

Raw umber

Ivory black

Titanium white

Brushes:

One ¾-inch bristle brush

Two small bristle brushes

One ½-inch soft-haired oil brush

One ¼-inch soft-haired oil brush

One No. 6 water-color brush

One No. 2 water-color brush

Palette Knife

other artists describe their methods

THESE BRIEF STATEMENTS BY SOME OF MY CELEBRATED COLLEAGUES WILL SHOW HOW differently artists approach the same medium. I feel certain that the reader will benefit from these notes, just as I have.

ARNOLD BLANCH: CASEIN PAINTING

When one attempts to write about a technique I think it should be prefaced by what is meant by technique. When using this word I mean the best means, at a particular time, of achieving an end. I do not believe there are classical or basic means that everyone should know or follow. It might be true that one person could benefit greatly by knowing the technique of Cennini, but others could be confused or frustrated in trying to apply this same knowledge to their technical problems in their particular time. In my contact with students I attempt to make clear that knowledge which does not lead to other knowledge is of little use in our fast moving world. The information a student receives from me can be of value only in proportion to the extent that it initiates avenues of research and invention.

In beginning a painting in casein, the approach depends to some degree upon the surface I am working on. If it is canvas or canvasboard, I almost always re-prime the surface in order to give the final painting more body. Before the prime is applied, I first sandpaper the canvas slightly. Then I prepare the prime, using 60 per cent Shiva Casein White with 40 per cent Permalba White. I mix these thoroughly with a palette knife and apply the prime with the same instrument—not too thickly, but enough to fill, or partially fill, the texture. I let this dry for a few days before painting on it. I use the same prime on plywood or wallboard panels, but apply it with a brush. When using illustration board, I first fasten the

108

board to a drawing board or stretchers, saving time and trouble that might otherwise occur from warping while the board is being primed.

I paint directly on the canvas or board without drawing first, but I have many notebooks filled with stenographic drawings or plans which may guide me. These renderings have originated from things I have seen, from things I have thought of, or from the end of my pencil without conscious thought. Since I do not always like to work on a white surface, I often apply a color tone to whatever surface I am working on. This tone varies according to my design. For example: If a red tone is used under black, the black becomes much richer than when painted over white; or if red is painted over black, it seems to have more weight than when painted over white. I paint the large forms first, and rather than painting up to the smaller forms I paint the small forms over and on top of the large ones. If I am dissatisfied with the drawing of my shapes, I will cut in and redraw with the background color.

Great brilliancy can be built up by painting certain forms white, then, after they are dry, staining them with thin pigment or India ink.

Beginners usually have difficulty because they use too little paint to cover well; they mix too little paint, or try to put it on too thinly. They also run into difficulties when they try to paint over a color before it is dry or when their palette is too small or dirty.

I find that sable brushes are more sympathetic than bristles. I use the flat as well as the round variety, and both small water-color brushes and the long-haired ones called liners. For painting large surfaces, a 1½- or 2-inch ox-hair brush is useful. At times I find unorthodox tools more useful than brushes, and I often use rags, sandpaper, a rubber roller, and stencils to achieve interesting effects.

I have tried various casein colors, but seem to prefer those made by Shiva.

AARON BOHROD: GOUACHE PAINTING

The opaque, heavily bodied variety of water color has always seemed to me to have greater potentialities than transparent color. I have used casein, tube tempera, and the recently developed pigment containing wax (Tri-tec) in my versions of the gouache technique. Casein I find to be a little chalkier than tube tempera, though much more durable. Tri-tec, with water as the medium, has the added advantage of attaining a moderate gloss under cloth rubbing, so that glass may not be required in the framing process.

As quickly as possible I try to make a tentative statement with my gouache material, establishing the main outlines of the design within the area of my board.

Then almost flat pattern masses are washed in thinly to blueprint the course of the finished painting. I like to work over a tentative underpainting of transparent water color or of thinly brushed opaque color. This allows my final painting, which naturally has breaks of surface, to rest on a colored tone, obviating the disturbing flecks of white paper which would otherwise show through and throw out of kilter a well-ordered design. The final stage of painting may proceed more leisurely, with the pigment worked by brush, palette knife, pointed sticks or other instruments, to attain varied textures and arrangements of color.

Many students miss the charm an opaque water color can attain by drawing their design carefully in pencil before they begin to paint. They then engage in the constraining process of filling in outlines. On the other hand, working from a more or less comprehensive sketch for reference, one may take a bold approach by establishing broad underlying shapes and then refining the larger masses with secondary forms and bringing the whole into integrated realization through judicious balance of textured and bland areas. This latter method is, I believe, a preferable approach. Shaping, constructing, drawing with color keeps the design, though opaque, limpid and vital.

AARON BOHROD: MIXED MEDIUM

I have found a great deal of pleasure in experimenting with a medium which combines the use of wax crayons, transparent water colors, and colored inks.

This mixed-medium process is usually started over a fairly comprehensive pen-and-ink drawing. I work with an ordinary fountain pen in my sketch books, and these still afford (after many drawings have been used as the basis for opaque water color, oil, or encaustic paintings) some designs which can stand up, I hope, as minor art manifestations when developed with this mixed medium. Because on-the-spot drawings often state only subject information, most of them must be re-drawn for compositional tightening and fuller expression.

I use a washable fountain-pen ink, usually a warm brown, for my basic drawing on paper or illustration board. Employing the resist-process, I lay in areas of wax crayon over the sketch. The areas heavily covered with the wax crayon will repel the color washes which are to be applied later, while the areas lightly laid with crayon will allow the color wash to penetrate, making a broken color half-tone of high luminosity. Those areas which are relatively untouched by wax will, of course, receive the fullest impact of the wash.

In this process only the light-colored or pigmentless crayons are useful. And only dark, rich washes offer the required contrasting tones which make the combination work.

After the crayon tones have been laid over the pen-and-ink drawing and I have double-checked to see that the areas which are to be lightest are covered with enough wax to resist the washes, I brush over the entire surface. Either one tone or, better, a changeable warm and cool color variation may be used. Water color or colored inks can be employed. Inks have a satisfying, dark, clean tone; water color has the advantage, possibly, of greater permanence.

When the surface has dried, excess crayon is scraped away with a razor blade to remove the local stain that overlying color imparts to the waxed portions of the drawing. By scraping I also modify the obvious and greasy look of some of the crayon area. A heavier color ink line may be needed to reinforce the design here and there. Though colorful, the design is often vague and needs decisive accents to strengthen it.

Mixed-medium painting on thin papers may be mounted with good paste on a stiff construction board and then rubbed and polished down with a wax varnish. Dorland's wax medium is good for this purpose. The wax finish eliminates the necessity of using glass in framing. When this kind of painting is placed under glass a film is formed which causes an unpleasant interposing veil.

With more widespread use of this medium, perhaps an enterprising color maker will produce wax crayons in more subtle tones than are now available, and with pigments superior to the quality found in the children's crayon sets which must be utilized.

Different effects may be obtained by using crayons which are more or less waxy, or more or less chalky, in their composition. A good deal of experimentation is necessary to attain control, to avoid total dependence on the lucky accident which must always play some part in the process. Experimental charts with heavy and light applications of crayon, as well as various color washes, are very useful for the worker in this medium.

Different kinds of papers also play an important role in offering textural variety. The rougher sheets allow a more rugged effect, best suited to large scale work, while more delicate effects can be obtained on smoother surfaces. In all instances paper should have some, even if only a little, tooth, since crayon will not adhere properly to surfaces which are too glossy.

For lightening inked tones which have gone too dark, and for drawing a light line through a work, a clothing bleach can be used. The bleach functions as an ink eradicator.

When a work in this medium has been accomplished with a good measure of control, the results are very rewarding. A luminosity results which has a peculiar impact impossible to attain through a built-up medium process. The signal drawback is the possible impermanence of these works. If materials were improved, especially in the basic crayon product, this lack of assurance would be overcome. However, a good deal of the total impact relies as much on what the overlying wash tones do *not* do as on what they do accomplish. The permanency of the crayon pigment plays a lesser part than its waxy properties, and even if all color were to fade out after many years, the essential drawing effect would still remain.

FEDERICO CASTELLON: RESIST-INK TECHNIQUE

The resist-ink medium is so named because of the property of heavy gouache or poster color of absorbing ink without allowing it to penetrate through to the surface of the paper or board. It is perhaps more familiarly known as the "wash-off" technique, the unflattering title commonly used in the field of commercial art. The materials needed are a few more than those used for water colors—one jar each of white and black poster color, India ink, and a jar of picture wax.

I have found from experience that water-color board of good quality rag is preferable to paper. Sketch your composition on the board in pencil line. If you feel the need of some key for the tonal composition it is advisable that you make a separate small sketch of your blacks and whites and shading to guide you; for the final step in the process is to rub the painting with picture wax, and if the painting has been shaded with pencil, the penciling will smudge the drawing and destroy the brilliance of the colors.

The second step on the painting is to block out the whites. For this step, add the barest touch of tone to the white poster paint to facilitate the painting on the white board; otherwise the white poster color on white board will be difficult to follow. Keep the consistency of the paint flowing but quite thick, so that it is absolutely opaque on the board. Wherever you want white, apply this slightly toned poster color, using your brush freely; and make very free use of the dry brush effect to enrich the textural quality of the painting.

After you have filled in all those areas which you want white or light gray (obtained through the use of the dry brush), the third step begins. Paint in your black poster color, using the same consistency of color and method of brush work as you used with the white poster color. The black should cover all areas which are eventually to be medium gray or darker gray (with the use of the dry brush), for in the process this black color will wash off to become gray. Gradations of color can be obtained through the technique of dry brush, since it is painting in the negative at this point. After some practice, shading should become more facile.

112

When all of the poster color is thoroughly dry, it is time for the fourth step. The object of this step is to cover the entire surface of the painting, poster color included, with a coat of India ink, without lifting or dissolving the color. The waterproof ink must not penetrate through to the surface of the board. Other than using an air brush or spray with the India ink, the best method is to fill the brush well and still manage not to leave on the painting puddles which might dissolve the poster color. In brushing on the ink, try to run the brush fast enough so that it passes over the entire area of poster color before it begins to soften. Avoid rubbing or going over areas that are too wet with ink. Deftly touch up any spot left without India ink after the area surrounding the spot is dry.

The fifth step is to wash the entire surface of the painting under running water. All of the poster color will wash off, leaving the white board where the white poster paint had been and a gray wash where the black poster paint was used. The India ink, being waterproof, will have remained black. The poster colors will have absorbed the ink without allowing its penetration to the surface of the board.

After this, you may either leave the composition as a black and white drawing or continue to build it up with water color. In this sixth step, you may discover that after several washes of water color, no matter how transparent the water colors are, a slight film will begin to dull the blacks considerably. However, when all of the color is finally on, apply the picture wax to the composition with your fingers and rub it hard with a lint-free cloth. This will restore the full luminosity and richness to your colors and give full depth to your blacks.

DORIS LEE: GOUACHE PAINTING

I have sketch books filled with little pencil sketches and notes of things I have seen or ideas I have had.

When starting a gouache, I attach illustration board to my drawing board with thumbtacks. Then, using the color in about the consistency of light cream, I wash in the large background areas. The shapes of these areas must always be related to that of the entire picture. When this is done and the paint has already dried, sometimes it is good to spray water over the whole area. This gives you the opportunity of blending edges of color and imparting various textures while the whole thing is wet. After the surface is thoroughly dry again, I paint in the smaller shapes directly over this background. For these shapes or subjects I like to use purer, brighter pigment and often black and white.

For me, it is better to paint several pictures and select the best than to paint too cautiously or overwork any one painting.

113

Most of my paintings are done in Shiva casein, which I recommend as an excellent medium for the student. It can be used either thickly, in opaque or impasto, or thinly as in a transparent water color. Frequently I use a combination of the two, building up a solidity of form with the opaques, then glazing over when dry to add additional color and light. (Glazing refers to a lightly brushed transparent wash. It is not a difficult technique; but does require clean color, clean water, and a clean brush—preferably a wide sable brush.) Added to these two basic types of application, there are very interesting possibilities in the use of such tools as the palette knife, a single-edged razor blade, and the pointed end of the brush-handle for applying thickness of pigment and developing texture. And, of course, with casein, one layer of paint can be applied over another and light color can be applied at any time, so that, in general, this medium does not have the "tightrope-walking" difficulties of transparent water color, where the paper is the only white.

I use the following colors:

Titanium white	Burnt umber
Cadmium yellow light *or* lemon yellow	Light red
Cadmium yellow medium	Indian red
Cadmium red light *or* vermilion	Cobalt blue
Cadmium red deep	Prussian blue *or* Thalo blue
Alizarin crimson	*or* Shiva blue
Yellow ocher	Ultramarine blue
Raw sienna	Ponsol blue
Burnt sienna	Viridian
Raw umber	Ivory black

You will notice that viridian is the only green listed, and I strongly recommend that the student learn to mix his own greens. Nothing is worse than an "out-of-the-tube green" summer landscape, and you will find that by mixing your own greens you will get a beautiful variety. As a starter, try mixing each of the colors in one of these columns with each of those in the other:

Cadmium yellow light *or* lemon yellow		Viridian
	Mixed with	Prussian blue
Cadmium yellow medium	each of	Cobalt blue
Yellow ocher	these	Ultramarine blue
Raw sienna	colors;	Ponsol blue

114

This type of cross-mixture practice is also very valuable for discovering a variety of cool and warm reds, cool and warm grays, and so on. Bear in mind that, just as a pianist knows the possibilities of the eighty-eight keys of the piano, the painter should know the range of his palette.

Casein is a very permanent medium that adheres to a wide variety of surfaces. (Incidentally, it also adheres very strongly to your brushes, so that it is necessary to wash your brushes thoroughly when through painting.) I use illustration board, fairly smooth but with some "tooth" to it, extra heavy sketch paper, and Masonite for my painting surfaces.

For a basic set of brushes, I recommend the following:

> One large 2- to 3-inch brush
> One 1-inch white bristle brush
> One ¾-inch white bristle brush
> One wide sable wash brush
> One smaller, pointed sable brush

The large brush is for laying in big areas of opaque color, and the best quality 2- or 3-inch brush obtainable at a hardware store will do very nicely. When buying brushes of any kind, always get the best quality that you can afford, because a few good brushes are a much better investment in the long run than a bunch of "weak" ones.

Palette knives come in a wide variety of sizes. I advise getting the "step-down" variety, one large one with rounded point, and one small one with a sharper point.

I recommend a large palette and have found that the enamel trays from gas ranges are ideal. These can generally be obtained at a small cost from second-hand stores. If you are going outdoors to paint, another easily transported palette, or set of palettes, is a nest of six pie tins. Use a generous-sized receptacle for water, such as a screw-top Mason jar. If you are working indoors it is easy to change the water as soon as it gets muddy. Always be sure to change the water as often as necessary, because clean water is an important factor in your painting procedure. If you are painting outdoors, I advise taking along two pint jars of water so that you have a spare clean supply.

Incidentally, I have found that a large fishing-tackle box makes an ideal receptacle for transporting all my material, which includes, besides the jars, paints, brushes, pens and ink, charcoal, pastels, fixative, blower, and tissues. I usually work seated on the ground, and use my tackle-box as an easel, tipping my board against it. If you are buying a conventional easel, I recommend the aluminum type with the additional water-color attachment that tilts to any desired angle.

115

In recent years, in addition to painting in casein, I have worked a good deal in mixed media: that is, various combinations of pen and ink, ink applied with brush, and fixed charcoal, combined with transparent and opaque casein and pastel. Specifically, some of these combinations are:

Pen line and transparent
Pen line and opaque
Ink applied with brush and opaque
Pen line and pastel
Opaque over fixed charcoal

This latter medium I find excellent for winter landscapes, as I can work this way conveniently in my car, fix my drawing, and complete it in the studio.

Some of my best work has been done in mixed media, and I recommend that the student try his hand at it. Several years ago I conducted a class in mixed media at the Kansas City Art Institute, and some very interesting work was produced. Working with mixed media helps the student develop his drawing and painting at one and the same time, which is as it should be.

Here are the additional materials which you will need for mixed media.

Pen: I use a regular fountain pen with a broad, flexible nib.

Ink: Higgin's Eternal Ink, which can be used in a fountain pen. To assure a free flow of ink the pen should be flushed out occasionally with clean water.

Brush: A small Japanese or Chinese pointed brush, the type which has a bamboo handle and fitted top.

Charcoal: French Vine is excellent.

Fixatives: Both charcoal and pastel are needed.

Fixative blower

Pastels: The large sets of pastels are very complete as to range of color but are quite expensive and contain many colors that I don't use, so I prefer to go to a large art store and pick out the colors I want from the pastel stock drawers.

Remember that drawing represents the "bones of painting," so draw all you can. Carry your painting and drawing along together, and if you're temporarily "color-blinded," hearken to the words of the great colorist, Henri Matisse. When he was asked to give some advice to the young artists, he said: "Draw, draw, and then draw some more." It is a hundred times better to "get your hooks into the thing" by establishing your drawing and composition and working into or over this than it is to attempt a perfect, purist-technique water color. You will gain a lot more by a painting plus drawing study than you will by following the will-o'-the-wisps of the "anyone can paint a water color" or "water color made easy" school that has been rather overdone of late.

Opposite: *Detail of Casein painting by Arnold Blanch.*

Two steps showing a painting in resist-ink process. Aaron Bohrod.

"Mending Nets." Mixed media, water color and ink. Bruce Mitchell.

"The Gladiator and the Tourist." Contemporary, pastel, pen and ink. Federico Castellon.

"Washerwomen." Resist-ink. Federico Castellon.

"Winter in the City." Gouache. Aaron Bohrod.

"Around the Bend." Gouache. Bruce Mitchell.

"Feeding the Birds." Casein. Arnold Blanch.

Opposite: *Gouache. Doris Lee.*

(Associated American Artists)

"Wild Flowers." Casein. Doris Lee.

"Mothers and Daughters." Adolf Dehn. Casein.

"Colorado Rockies." Adolf Dehn. Casein.

"Haitian Panorama." Adolf Dehn. Water color.

"Water Hole, Key West." Adolf Dehn. Gouache.

"The Clean and the Unclean." Adolf Dehn. Casein.